T0150490

The Lives of Angels

The Lives of Angels

Emanuel Swedenborg

Translated by George F. Dole and Lisa Hyatt Cooper
Introduction by Grant Schnarr

SWEDENBORG FOUNDATION
West Chester, Pennsylvania

Excerpts from *Heaven and Hell* were originally published in *Heaven and
Hell,* Emanuel Swedenborg, trans. George F. Dole (West Chester, PA:
Swedenborg Foundation, 2002).

Excerpts from *Secrets of Heaven* were originally published in *Secrets
of Heaven,* vols. 1–2, Emanuel Swedenborg, trans. Lisa Hyatt Cooper
(West Chester, PA: Swedenborg Foundation, 2010–12).

Excerpts from *Marriage Love* by Emanuel Swedenborg were taken from
an unpublished translation by George F. Dole and are used by permission.

Cover art: Sections of the twelve-foot transparency, *Figures Walking in a Parkland* (watercolor and
gouache on translucent Whatman paper), by Louis Carrogis de Carmontelle (French, 1717–1806).
Carmontelle invented his *rouleau transparent,* an ancestor of modern cinema, as a band of scenes
unrolled within a backlit box and displayed as a contiguous, illuminated sequence.
Image reproduced courtesy of J. Paul Getty Museum.

Edited by Morgan Beard
Design and typesetting by Karen Connor

Printed in the United States of America

Swedenborg Foundation
320 North Church Street • West Chester, PA 19380
www.swedenborg.com

CONTENTS

INTRODUCTION

OUR FASCINATION WITH ANGELS goes back to the very roots of the recorded history of religion, from Zoroastrianism, Judaism, and Islam to modern-day Christianity, from ancient philosophers such as Aristotle to contemporary authors such as Doreen Virtue, Jacky Newcomb, Anthony DeStephano, and even the renowned preacher and spiritual leader Billy Graham. Angels have been described as powerful beings with the desire and ability to help us, as guardians against evil, and as messengers from the Divine, touching our lives through gentle whispers or, as some have experienced, through miraculous encounters.

What fascinates us about angels? What makes us want to learn more and imagine more about them, to feel more connected to these supernatural beings? My experience as a pastor and spiritual writer, my studies, and my countless conversations with people about angels have shown me that our attraction to angels is based on their core qualities. One factor is certainly their beauty, as depicted in religious and spiritual art and described in the revelations of the great world religions. This beauty goes so much deeper than is depicted on the surface. It is the angels' inner quality, the light that pours from their core, that radiates and surrounds them as they touch our lives.

What is the quality at the heart of these beings that creates such a yearning within us to draw closer to them? What bonds angels to us, to God, and to one another? I believe the answer is love. Angels are the embodiment of love—love perfected, love in action. They are the light bringers, the love bearers, from the Source of light and love. In both Old Testament Hebrew and New Testament Greek, the word "angel" means "messenger." In all they do, not just in word but in deed, they fulfill the role of ambassadors of God, carrying the message of divine love. They are ambassadors of Love. Their total embodiment of love is what makes angels beautiful and powerful beyond measure. It is what gives them the ability to inspire, guide, and protect us, to tenderly lead us to what is higher than ourselves.

Emanuel Swedenborg, the eighteenth-century scientist and theologian, describes angels as perfect human expressions of divine love. He means "human" in its highest sense, as reflecting the source of humanity itself, the lone being who might carry the title of the Divine Human. In *Divine Providence* (paragraph 46), Swedenborg says that "we are because God is." We are human because God is divinely human. But Swedenborg doesn't stop there. He claims that you and I were born to become angels! Over the course of the many years when he was in communication with the denizens of heaven and hell, Swedenborg learned that the purpose of creation is for human beings to be gradually perfected, in this world and the next, in order to create heaven. He reported that the celestial beings we call "angels" are not supernatural beings, but humans who once lived on this earth. Everyone who learns to truly love others, growing in the wisdom that accompanies love, becomes an angel of heaven. We continue that growth in communion with God and in community with other angels for eternity.

In his theological works, Swedenborg not only states that we have the capacity to become angels, and that this is God's intent, but he sets forth what some have called the most comprehensive description of heaven and of the lives of angels in heaven. He tells us that in heaven we don't just sit around on clouds playing harps or singing in heavenly choirs praising God forever and ever. Who would want that for eternity? Rather, angels honor God with active lives of service, by doing what they love most, what they do best, and what brings joy and fulfillment to others as well as to themselves. The joy in heaven is overflowing, as Jesus said: "Give, and it will be given to you. A good measure, pressed down, shaken together and running over, will be poured into your lap. For with the measure you use, it will be measured to you" (Luke 6:38).

In the following pages you will learn how this joy comes about, what angels do, where and how they live, what kinds of relationships they have, and the nature and origin of the love that shines in their lives. In some pages, Swedenborg tells stories of events he saw in the other world, while in others he simply recounts what he was taught. His descriptions of angelic life more than fulfill our fascination with angels; they give us hope and comfort, even excitement, about what heavenly life may be waiting for all of us.

This book is about angels, but it also about you: Swedenborg describes a path that all human beings are capable of following if they choose. He tells us that God sends angels to watch over us, to guide us, to share love and wisdom, and to give us the opportunity to grow spiritually. The purpose of creation, he teaches, is a heaven created from the human race. You are a part of that purpose. You were born to be an angel.

—GRANT SCHNARR
Author of *The Guardian Angel Diary* and *Ghost Brother Angel*

The Lives of Angels

Our Ideas of Angels

THE JOYS OF HEAVEN

I EXPECT THAT MANY PEOPLE who read the following stories will think that they are figments of my imagination. I give you my word, though, that they are not figments. They are things that actually happened, things I have actually seen. I did not see them when my mind was asleep, either, but when I was completely awake. The Lord has graciously disclosed himself to me and commissioned me to convey information about a new church, which is what *the New Jerusalem* in the book of Revelation means. For this purpose, he has opened the deeper levels of my mind and my spirit, which has enabled me to be with angels in the spiritual world even while I am with people in this physical world. This has been going on for twenty-five years now.

One day I saw an angel flying under the eastern sky, holding a trumpet to his mouth and sounding it toward the north, the west, and the south. He was wearing a mantle that streamed out behind him as he flew and had on a belt blazing with brilliant red and blue gems. He was flying prone and landed gently not far from where I was standing. Then he stood up and walked around, and when he saw me he came over toward me. I was in the spirit, and in the spirit was standing on a hill in the southern region. When he was near enough, I spoke to him and asked, "What's going on? I heard the sound of your trumpet and saw you coming down through the air."

He answered, "I have been sent to convene people who are most admired for their learning, are most insightful, and who have the highest reputation for wisdom among those from the Christian world who are in this general region. They are to meet right on this hill where you are and say what they really think, presenting the thoughts, analysis, and wisdom about *heavenly joy and eternal happiness* they had had when they were living in the world. I've been asked to do this because when some newcomers from the world were admitted to our community, which is in the east, they reported that hardly anyone in the whole Christian world knows what heavenly joy and eternal happiness are and therefore what heaven is. This seemed incredible to my friends and companions, and they told me to go down, sound the call, and gather the wisest people that were in the world of spirits (which is where all mortals arrive together after leaving the physical world). We want to find out for sure, from the testimony of many individuals, whether it is true that Christians are in such darkness, such benighted ignorance, about their future life." He added, "Wait a bit and you will see some groups of scholars headed in this direction. The Lord has provided a hall for them."

I waited, and in half an hour I saw two groups coming from the north, two from the west, and two from the south. When they arrived, the angel with the trumpet brought them into the hall that had been provided and they took places assigned to them according to their regions. There were six groups or sets, plus a seventh to the east, which the others did not see because the light was in their eyes.

Once they were assembled, the angel introduced the purpose of the meeting and asked the groups to present their wisdom, one at a time, about *heavenly joy and eternal happiness.* Then each group clustered in a circle, face to face, to refresh their memories about the concepts they had adopted in the former world and to critique them, and then to present their findings once they had finished their consultation.

After they had conferred, the first group from the north said that heavenly joy and eternal happiness were the very same thing as living in heaven. This meant that everyone who got into heaven was completely caught up in its festivities, just the way everyone who comes to a wedding gets caught up in its festivities. "Heaven is up there where we see it, isn't it? So it's in a place, and that's where we'll find bliss upon bliss and pleasure upon pleasure, there and nowhere else. People are caught up with every perception of their minds and every sensation of their bodies because of the overflowing joy of the place itself when they are in heaven. Heavenly happiness, then, which is eternal, is simply admission into heaven, and this admission is by divine grace."

After this speech, the second group from the north gave the following interpretation based on their wisdom. "Heavenly joy and eternal happiness are nothing more nor less than the utterly delightful company of angels and the absolutely charming conversations with them. As a result, people's faces are always open and cheerful, and there is infectious laughter on everyone's lips in response to charming phrases and pleasantries. What else is heavenly joy but variations on this theme to eternity?"

Then the third group, the first group of sages from the western region, expressed their fondest thoughts by saying, "What are heavenly joy and eternal happiness but banquets with Abraham, Isaac, and Jacob at tables loaded with elegant, rich foods and exquisite vintage wines? Then after the banquets, there will be games and troupes of young men and women dancing to the rhythms of orchestras, with interludes of sweetest song. As evening comes, there will be presentations by actors, then more banquets, and so on, day after day forever."

Next, the fourth group, the second from the western region, gave voice to their opinion. "We've come up with several concepts of heavenly joy that appeal to us. We've discussed various joys and compared them to each other, and have decided that heavenly joys are the joys of a garden paradise. What is heaven but a paradise that stretches from east to west and from south to north? It is full of fruit trees and lovely flowers. The glorious tree of life is at its center, and the blessed, all decked out with the most fragrant of flowers, sit around it sampling subtly flavored fruits. These fruits and flowers are touched daily by the breath of constant springtime, so they are constantly born and reborn with infinite variety; and in response to their constant birth and flowering and the constant springtime climate, the souls of the blessed are constantly renewed. They cannot help but gather and inhale new joys with every passing day. This restores them to the flower of youth and then to that primeval state into which Adam and his wife Eve were created. So it restores them to an Eden raised from earth to heaven."

The fifth group (the first group of insightful people from the southern region) came out with the following pronouncement. "Heavenly joys and eternal happiness are simply supreme power and limitless wealth. These yield glory beyond that of royalty and utterly dazzling brilliance. By looking at people who have enjoyed these blessings in the world, we can tell that these are the joys of heaven and that the constant experience of these joys is eternal happiness. Above all, there is the fact that the blessed in heaven will reign with the Lord and will themselves be kings and princes because they are the children of the One who is King of Kings and Lord of Lords. They will sit on thrones, and angels will minister to them. We can tell how glorious heaven is from the fact that in the New Jerusalem, the very picture of heaven's beauty, each gate will be a single pearl, the streets will be made of pure gold [Revelation 21:21], and the foundations of the walls will be precious gems [Revelation 21:19–20]. So everyone who is accepted into heaven will have a mansion gleaming with gold and gems, and will have a place in an orderly hierarchy. Since we know that joys are inherent in these blessings, that they are full of happiness, and since they are God's unconditional promises, as far as we can see this is the only possible source of a supremely happy state of heavenly life."

Next, the sixth group (the second from the southern region) spoke up. "Heavenly joy and heaven's eternal happiness are nothing but the perpetual glorification of God, a special Sunday that lasts forever, an absolutely blissful worship service with songs and shouts of praise. This brings about a constant raising of the heart toward God in complete trust that our prayers and praise are accepted because of the divine generosity that blesses them." Some of the group added the thought that this glorification would be accompanied by splendid lights and the finest incense and most impressive processions, led by the high priest with a great trumpet, followed by bishops and acolytes great and small, and lastly men carrying palm branches and women holding golden images in their hands.

The seventh group, which was not seen because the light was in the others' eyes, came from the eastern part of heaven. They were angels from the same community as the angel with the trumpet. When in their own heaven they had heard that not a single soul in the Christian world knew what heavenly joy and eternal happiness were, they said to each other, "There's no way this can be true! How can there be such darkness, such a mental coma among Christians! We should go down and hear for ourselves whether this is true; and if it is true, it is truly appalling!"

Then the angels said to the angel with the trumpet, "You are aware that all those who have longed for heaven and have had definite thoughts about its joys are led into those imagined joys after death. Once they have experienced what these joys are really like and have discovered that they reflect only the baseless speculations of their own minds and the wanderings of their own imaginations, they are led out of them and are taught. This happens in the world of spirits to many individuals who have given serious thought to heaven in their former life and who have formed fixed opinions about heaven's joys on the basis of their own desires."

On hearing this, the angel with the trumpet said to the six groups that had been assembled from the sages of the Christian world, "Follow me, and I will lead you into your joys, and therefore into heaven."

After saying this, the angel took the lead. The first group that followed was the group of people who had convinced themselves that heavenly joys were nothing but delightful company and charming conversations. The angel brought them to a gathering, in the northern district, of people whose concept of heavenly joys in the former world had been precisely that.

There was a spacious house there where these people met. The house had more than fifty rooms, distinguished by different topics of conversation. In some rooms they were talking about what they had seen and heard in public gatherings and in the streets; in some they were talking about love and the opposite sex, with so many witticisms that every face in the group wore a broad grin; in some rooms they were sharing the latest from the court, departments of state, the administration, and various leaks from confidential councils, along with calculations and conjectures about what the outcome would be; in some they talked about business, in some about scholarly subjects, in some about matters of civic strategy and moral living, in some about issues in the church and its sects; and so on. I was enabled to look into the house, and I saw people scurrying from room to room, looking for the groups that shared their own taste and therefore their own delight. In the groups themselves I saw three kinds of people. Some were panting to speak, some were bursting with questions, and some were eager to listen.

The house had four doors, one in each direction, and I noticed that quite a few people were leaving the groups, hurrying to get out. I followed some to the eastern door and found people sitting next to the door with downcast faces, so I went up to them and asked why they were sitting there so sadly. They answered, "The doors of this house are kept closed against those who are trying to leave. This is the third day since we came in, and we have spent the time living the life of our dreams, in discussion groups. We are so tired of the constant talk that we can scarcely stand to hear the faintest murmur of it, so out of total boredom we found our way to this door and knocked. The response, though, has been that the doors of this house do not open to people who want to leave, only to people who want to come in. 'Stay here and enjoy the delights of heaven!' We gather from this that we will be staying here forever, and that is a profoundly depressing thought. Now our chests are beginning to feel constricted, and we are becoming more and more dismayed."

The angel then addressed them. "This state is the death of your joys, the joys you thought were the only heavenly ones. In fact, though, they are nothing but fringe benefits of heaven." They asked the angel, "What is heavenly joy, then?" and the angel answered simply, "It is the pleasure of doing something that benefits both yourselves and others. The pleasure of this kind of service gets its essential substance from love and its visible form from wisdom. The pleasure of a service that arises from love through wisdom is the soul and life of all heavenly joys.

"There are the most delightful gatherings in the heavens, gatherings that bring joy to angels' minds, lift their spirits, warm their hearts, and refresh their bodies. They enjoy these gatherings, though, after they've been doing useful things in their various posts and in their jobs. This usefulness is the source of the soul and life within all their happiness and pleasure; but if you take away that soul or life, these extra joys gradually cease to be joys at all. First they become matters of indifference, then they seem worthless, and finally they become depressing and worrisome."

On this, the door opened and the people who had been sitting by it leapt up and fled the house. Each went to her or his post or job, and they were revitalized.

Next, the angel turned to the people who had come up with the idea that heavenly joys and eternal happiness were banquets with Abraham, Isaac, and Jacob, then games and shows after the banquets, then more banquets, and so on forever. "Follow me," he said, "and I will take you to the happiness of your joys."

He then led them through a grove into a field that was paved with planks. There were tables on the planks, fifteen on each side. When they asked why there were so many tables, the angel said that the first table was for Abraham, the second for Isaac, and the third for Jacob, and that beyond these there were tables lined up for each of the twelve apostles. On the other side there were just as many tables for their wives. The first three tables were for Abraham's wife Sarah, Isaac's wife Rebecca, and Jacob's wives Leah and Rachel. The twelve other tables were for the wives of the twelve apostles.

Before long, we could see that the tables were fully set with serving dishes, and that the spaces between the dishes were decorated with little pyramids of appetizers. The diners were standing around waiting to see the heads of each table, and in a little while the expectant crowd saw them enter in procession, Abraham first and the apostles last. Each went straight to his or her own table and reclined on the couch at its head; whereupon they said to the people who were standing, "Come join us." Then the men reclined to dine with the men and the women with the men's wives, and they cheerfully and respectfully began to eat and drink.

After the meal the elders left and the festivities started—boys' and girls' choirs, followed by plays. Once these were over, they were summoned to banquets again, but with the requirement that they should dine with Abraham on the first day, Isaac on the second, and Jacob on the third, Peter on the fourth, James on the fifth, John on the sixth, and Paul on the seventh, then with the rest in order until the fifteenth day, at which point they would start a new round of feasts in the same sequence but with different seating arrangements. This would continue to eternity.

After this, the angel called the group together and said to them, "All the people you saw at the tables had the same imaginary idea as you about heaven's joys and the eternal happiness that they bring. These banquet scenarios have been arranged and allowed by the Lord in order to show them the futility of their notions and wean them away from them. The eminent gentlemen you saw at the heads of the tables were old actors, mostly rustic types with beards, who were particularly prosperous and proud of it. They have been caught up in the fantasy that they actually are those ancient individuals. But follow me to the exits from this area."

When they did, they saw fifty people here and another fifty there, stuffed to the point of nausea. Those who had been feasting could not wait to get back to the familiar surroundings of their own homes, some to their chores, some to their businesses, and some to their jobs; but many were being held back by the grove's guards and questioned about their days of banqueting. "Have you dined with Peter and Paul yet? It's rude to leave before you do. You should be ashamed of yourselves." Many of them were answering, "We are stuffed to the brim with our joys. The food has become tasteless, and our taste buds have dried up. Our stomachs are rebelling. We cannot stand even the touch of food. We have spent days and nights in this overindulgence, and we beg you to let us leave." Once they were given permission, they dashed home breathlessly, as fast as they could run.

The angel then gathered the group and told them about heaven as they walked back. "There are food and drink in heaven just as there were on earth. There are banquets and parties. For the upper classes there are tables with the most elegant banquets, with refreshments and delicacies to enliven and restore their spirits. There are games and plays as well, and concerts and recitals, all performed to perfection. These provide joys for angels, but not happiness. Happiness must be within the joys if the joys are to bring happiness. It is the happiness within the joys that makes them joyful, that enriches and maintains them so that they don't become trivial and distasteful. Angels get this happiness from the good that is done in their individual tasks.

"In the heartfelt desires of all angels there is a kind of hidden current that draws their minds toward some action. This action serves to set their minds at rest and give them a sense of satisfaction; and that satisfaction and calm create a state of mind that is open to accept from the Lord a love of service. Accepting this love is the heavenly happiness that is the life within those joys of angels that have just been described.

"In its essence, heavenly food is nothing but love, wisdom, and service combined, that is, service by means of wisdom arising from love. So everyone in heaven is given food for the body in keeping with the level of function that she or he performs—fine cuisine if the function is of great importance, conventional but delicious food if the function is moderately important, and coarse food if the function is merely ordinary, with none for the lazy."

Then the angel summoned the group of so-called sages who had believed that heavenly joys and a consequent eternal happiness were to be found in supreme power and limitless wealth. They had dreams of imperial glory and visions of dazzling brilliance. They based this on statements in the Word that they would be kings and princes, that they would reign with Christ forever, and that angels would serve them, among other things.

"Follow me," the angel said to them, "and I will introduce you to your joys." He led them to a gallery of columns and pyramids. There was an unpretentious building in front of it that gave entry to the gallery. He led them through it, and they saw twenty people here and another twenty there, waiting. Abruptly, someone in the guise of an angel came on the scene and said to them, "The path to heaven goes through this gallery. Stay here for a bit, and get ready, because the older of you are going to be kings and the younger will be up-and-coming princes."

At this point a throne appeared by each column, with a silk robe on it and a crown and scepter on each robe. Next to each pyramid appeared a seat raised some four feet above the floor, with a golden chain in each seat and a sash for an order of knighthood, fastened at the ends with little round diamonds.

Then there was a proclamation: "Come, put on your robes; take your seats and wait." So the older individuals promptly rushed to the thrones and the younger ones to the seats. They put on the robes and sashes and took their places. At that point, though, a kind of cloud seemed to rise up from the depths, and as it enveloped the people on their thrones and seats their faces began to puff up and their chests to expand. They were filled with the conviction that they were kings and princes now: the cloud was the aura of the illusion they were caught up in. Suddenly some young people seemed to fly to them from heaven and took up their places, two behind each throne and one behind each seat, ready to serve them. From time to time a herald would proclaim, "You, you kings and princes, wait just a little longer; your courts are being prepared in heaven. Your attendants and their assistants are just about to arrive, and they will lead you in." They kept waiting and waiting until their spirits were gasping for breath and they were worn out by their own eagerness.

After three hours of this, the heaven over them opened up. Some angels looked down, took pity on them, and said, "Why are you sitting there like idiots, playing make-believe? Your own pretenses have tricked you and have changed you from humans into idols. This is because you have taken to heart the notion that you are going to reign with Christ as kings and princes and that angels are going to minister to you. Have you forgotten the Lord's saying that anyone who wants to be great in heaven must become a servant [Matthew 20:27; Mark 10:44]? Learn then what it means to be kings and princes and to reign with Christ: it is being wise and helpful.

"The kingdom of Christ, or heaven, is made up of acts of service because the Lord loves everyone and wants what is best for everyone. What is best is service; and because the Lord provides that 'best,' or service, indirectly through angels, and in the world through individuals, he gives faithful servants a love of serving and the reward of that love, which is an inner bliss. This is eternal happiness.

"There are supreme powers and limitless wealth in heaven just as there are on earth. There are different realms and different forms of government; so there are positions that command greater and lesser power and respect. People on the highest levels do have palaces and courts whose richness and splendor transcend that of the palaces and courts of earthly emperors and kings. They are bathed in honor and splendor by virtue of the multitude of courtiers and ministers and attendants and their gorgeous apparel.

"However, the very highest positions are given to individuals who have taken to heart the well-being of the general public, and who give superficial, sensory attention to impressive splendor, and only because it encourages obedience. Further, since the well-being of the general public depends on everyone's having some useful function in the community as an inclusive body, and since all useful functions come from the Lord and are carried out by angels and people in apparent autonomy, we can see that this is what 'reigning with the Lord' means."

Once they had heard this message from heaven, the people who had been pretending to be kings and princes stepped down from their thrones and seats and dropped their scepters and crowns and robes. Then the cloud, the aura of their illusion, receded from them, and a bright cloud came over them with an aura of wisdom. This brought sanity back to their minds.

Then the angel came back to the gathering of sages from the Christian world and called the ones who had persuaded themselves that the joys of heaven and eternal happiness were the pleasures of a paradise. "Follow me," he said, "and I will lead you into paradise, your heaven, so that you can begin enjoying the bliss of your eternal happiness."

He led them through a tall entrance made of the interwoven branches and twigs of magnificent trees; and once they were inside he led them from place to place by winding paths. It was in fact a park at the first entryway to heaven where people are sent who in the world had believed that the whole of heaven was a single garden paradise because it is called "paradise" [Luke 23:43; 2 Corinthians 12:4; Revelation 2:7], people who had convinced themselves that after death there would be complete rest from their labors [Revelation 14:13]. Their idea of rest was nothing more than inhaling the spirit of pleasure, wandering among the roses, enjoying the most exquisite pressings from grapes, and holding wine parties—a life that was possible only in a heavenly garden paradise.

As they followed the angel, they saw an immense number of people of all ages, both male and female, sitting in the rose gardens in groups of three and groups of ten. They were weaving garlands to adorn the heads of the elders and the arms of the young and sashes for the chests of the children. Others were picking fruit from the trees and carrying them to their companions in baskets; some were pressing the juice from grapes, cherries, and berries into cups and cheerfully drinking; others were breathing in the fragrances given off far and wide by flowers and fruits and aromatic leaves; still others were singing charming songs to delight the hearing of everyone who heard them; some were sitting by fountains channeling the trickling waters into various forms; some were walking around chatting and scattering pleasantries; some were running, some playing, some dancing in measures and circles; some were going into gazebos to relax on couches; and there were other "pleasures of paradise" as well.

Once they had seen all this, the angel took the company around to various other places, finally coming to some people in a very lovely rose garden, surrounded by olive and orange and lemon trees. They were sitting there rocking back and forth, with their hands between their knees, in grief and in tears. The angel's company asked them, "Why are you sitting here like this?"

They answered, "This is the seventh day since we entered this paradise. When we first arrived, it seemed as though our minds had been raised right into heaven and plunged into the very center of the essence of happiness. After three days, though, these delights began to pall. They were being erased from our minds, fading from sense, and vanishing completely. Once our imaginary joys had died away, we were afraid we were going to lose every trace of delight in our lives. We were overcome by doubt about eternal happiness. Did it even exist? Then we wandered around through various paths and places looking for the entrance where we had come in. We wandered around and around and asked the people we met. Some of them told us that the entryway was not to be found because this garden paradise was an immense maze, designed in such a way that if you wanted to get out, you just went deeper and deeper into it. 'This means that there's nothing for you to do but stay here for eternity. You are at that midpoint where all joys are concentrated.'"

They went on to tell the angel's company, "We have now been sitting here for a day and a half, and since we have given up all hope of getting out, we have collapsed in this bed of roses. We look around at the abundance of olives and grapes and oranges and lemons, but the more we look, the more tired our sight is of seeing, our smell of smelling, and our taste of tasting. This why you see us so depressed, so sorrowful, and so tearful."

On hearing this, the angel guide said, "This mazelike park really is an entryway to heaven. I know the way out and I'll lead you."

In response to this, the people who had been sitting there leapt up, hugged the angel, and followed him and his company. As they walked along, the angel told them what heavenly joy and its consequent eternal happiness were. "They are not the pleasures of some garden paradise outside ourselves unless these are accompanied by the pleasures of a paradise inside ourselves. The pleasures of the outer paradise are simply physical, sensory pleasures, while the pleasures of the inner paradise are pleasures of the soul's own feelings. Unless the inner ones are within the outer, there is no heavenly life in the outer pleasures because there is no soul in them. If any pleasure has no corresponding soul within it, it eventually becomes tiresome and lifeless. It is more exhausting to the soul than work is.

"There are garden paradises everywhere in heaven, and angels take delight in them, too. To the extent that there is an inner delight of the soul, their delight is real."

This prompted everyone to ask, "What is this 'delight of the soul,' and where does it come from?"

"Delight of the soul comes from the love and wisdom the Lord gives us," the angel replied. "Since love is active, and since it acts through wisdom, the seat of them both is in activity; and the activity is service. This delight flows from the Lord into the soul and comes down through the higher and lower levels of the mind into all our physical senses. That is where it finds its fulfillment. That is why joy is joy. It lasts forever because it comes from the One who is eternal.

"You have seen the sights of paradise, and I assure you that there is nothing there, not the smallest leaf, that is not the product of a marriage of love and wisdom in service. So if that is what people are engaged in they are in a heavenly paradise, which means they are in heaven."

The angel guide then came back to the hall, this time to the group that had firmly convinced itself that heavenly joy and eternal happiness were constant glorification of God, a kind of eternal, endless Sunday. In the world, that is, they had believed that they would see God after death, and that the life of heaven was called a perpetual Sabbath because it consisted of worship of God. The angel said to them, "Follow me, and I will lead you to your joy."

He then took them to a small city with a temple at its center, a city where all the buildings bore signs saying that they were sacred halls. Within the city, they saw people coming from every corner of the surrounding territory. And among them there were several priests welcoming the arrivals, greeting them, and taking them by the hand to lead them to the temple gates and from there into the various halls surrounding the temple. They were introducing them to the perpetual worship of God, saying, "This city is a vestibule of heaven, and this temple is an entryway to a wondrous, vast temple in heaven where angels glorify God with prayers and praises to eternity. The rules both here and there call for you to begin by entering this temple and spending three days and three nights in it. After this prelude, you will go into the city's various buildings, each one a hall that we have consecrated. You will go from hall to hall and join with the congregations in praying, proclaiming, and reciting sermons. Be very careful, though, not to think about anything but holy, devout, and religious subjects, and not to talk about anything else with your companions."

The angel then led his company into the temple, which was packed full of a crowd of people who had been quite eminent in the world, along with many perfectly ordinary people. There were guards stationed at the doors to prevent anyone from leaving before staying for the three days. The angel said, "This is the second day since these people came in. Look at them carefully, and you will see how they are glorifying God."

They looked carefully and saw that most of them were asleep. The ones who were awake were yawning incessantly. Some of them, because of the constant raising of their thoughts toward God without letting them down toward their bodies, seemed to themselves and to others to have faces that were disconnected from their bodies. Some of them were seeing hallucinations because of their endless focus on abstractions. In short, they were all feeling stifled, spiritually exhausted from boredom, and were turned away from the pulpit. "This is too much for our ears!" they shouted. "No more sermons! Not another word! This noise is getting repulsive!" They then got up and rushed en masse to the doors, bursting through them, crowding in on the guards and pushing them back.

When they saw what was happening, the priests went after them and latched onto them, belaboring them with instruction, pleading with them, sighing, saying, "Celebrate this holy day! Glorify God! Consecrate yourselves! This vestibule of heaven is where we will prepare you for the eternal glorification of God in that wondrous, vast temple in heaven. This is where we are preparing you to enjoy eternal happiness!"

The crowd could not understand this at all. They were so dulled by two days of not thinking, of being divorced from their own private and public lives, that they could scarcely hear it. When they tried to push the priests away, though, the priests kept grabbing their arms and their clothing, trying vainly to force them toward the halls where the sermons would be given. They just kept shouting, "Let go of us! Even our bodies are feeling faint!"

As they said this, four men appeared wearing white robes and crowns. One of them had been an archbishop in the world, and the other three had been bishops; now all three had become angels. They called the priests together and addressed them: "We have seen you and your flock from heaven, and how you shepherd them. You are shepherding them straight into insanity! Don't you know what it means to glorify God? It means to bear the fruits of love, that is, to do the tasks of your position faithfully, honestly, and with care. This is what love of God and love of the neighbor really are. This is what holds society together and makes it worthwhile. This is how God is to be glorified, and secondarily with worship at regular intervals. Haven't you read the Lord's words, 'In this *is my Father glorified,* that you bear much fruit, and become my disciples' (John 15:8)? It's all very well for you priests to be occupied with formal worship, because that is your particular responsibility. You get respect, admiration, and reward from it. However, you would take to it no more than these people do if it were not for the respect and admiration and reward that are associated with your responsibility."

Once they had said this, the bishops ordered the doorkeepers to let everyone in and let everyone out. There are actually a great many people who can think of heavenly joy only as the perpetual worship of God, because they have not known anything about the actual state of heaven.

After this, the angel and his companions came back to the hall, which the other groups of sages had not yet left. There he summoned the ones who had believed that heavenly joy and eternal happiness were simply admission into heaven, and admission by divine grace. Then, they believed, they would experience joy. It would be just like going to the courts of royalty on festival days, or being guests at a wedding.

"Wait here a bit," the angel told them, "and I will sound my trumpet; and some individuals will come who are renowned for their wisdom regarding the spiritual aspects of the church."

In a few hours, nine men arrived, each wearing a laurel wreath as a sign of his reputation. The angel brought them into the meeting hall where everyone else was already gathered and in their presence spoke to the nine laureates. "I know that at your own request and in keeping with your own concepts you have been allowed to go up into heaven and that you have come back down to this lower region under heaven with a full knowledge of heaven's state. Tell us how heaven seemed to you."

They answered one at a time. The first said, "From early childhood until the end of my earthly life, I thought of heaven as the locus of all blessings, happiness, joys, delights, and pleasures. I thought that once I arrived there I would be immersed in the aura of this happiness. I would fill my lungs full with it. I would be like a groom on his wedding day entering the bedroom with his bride.

"That is the notion I had when I went up into heaven. I got past a first guard and then a second. When I came to the third, though, the chief guard said to me, 'Who are you, my friend?' I answered, 'Isn't this heaven? I've come up here because I wanted to so much. Please, let me in.'

"He did let me in, and I saw some angels in white robes. They surrounded me and looked me over, murmuring, 'Here is a new visitor who is not dressed for heaven.' When I heard this, I thought, 'This sounds like the man the Lord described as attending a wedding without being dressed in wedding garments' [Matthew 22:11–13]. So I said, 'Give me the right clothes.' They just laughed. Then someone from the court hurried up and said, 'Strip him naked, throw him out, and throw his clothes after him.' So I was thrown out."

The second laureate took his turn. "I held the same belief as he did, that if I were just let into heaven overhead, joys would surround me and I would breathe them in forever. My wish was granted; but when angels saw me, they ran away. 'What is this monstrosity?' they said to each other. 'How did this night bird get in here?' In fact, I felt as though I were becoming subhuman even though I had not actually changed. This happened to me as an effect of the heavenly atmosphere. Shortly, someone from the court came hurrying up with an order that two servants should take me out and lead me back to my own home by the way I had come. Once I was home, I seemed human to myself and to everyone else."

The third laureate said, "My own abiding notion of heaven was based on location and not on love; so when I arrived in this world, I felt a passionate desire for heaven. I saw some people headed upward and followed them. I was let in, but only for a few paces. I wanted my spirit to rejoice in what I thought were its joys and blessings, in the light of heaven, a light white as snow, whose essence was called wisdom, but my mind was filled with lethargy and my eyes with darkness, so that I began to go insane. Before long, the warmth of heaven, which parallels heaven's light and whose essence is called love, made my heart pound. I was overcome by anxiety and tormented with such inner pain that I threw myself right down flat on the ground. While I was lying there, some attendants came from the court with an order to carry me slowly back to my own light and to my own warmth; and once I arrived in them, I regained my spirit and my heart."

The fourth laureate then spoke up. "My idea of heaven was that it was just a place; I did not consider the notion of love. As soon as I arrived in the spiritual world, I asked some wise people whether I would be allowed to go up to heaven. They told me that anyone could go up, but that one had to be careful not to get thrown out. I laughed at the thought and started up, believing like everyone else that everyone in the whole world could welcome joys in their absolute fullness. In fact, though, once I was inside I could hardly breathe. I felt such pain, such agony in my head and my body, that I collapsed on the ground and writhed like a snake brought too close to a fire. I crawled all the way to the edge and threw myself over. Later, I was picked up by some passersby and taken to an inn, where I regained my health."

The other five told their remarkable stories of ascent into heaven, comparing the way their states changed to the situation of fish lifted up into the air or birds into the ether. They said that after these trying experiences they no longer craved heaven. All they wanted was the companionship of people like themselves, wherever that might be found; they knew that in the world of spirits, where they now were, all are prepared in advance, the good for heaven and the evil for hell. Once they are prepared, they see paths open up for them to communities of the like-minded souls with whom they will live to eternity. They start along these paths cheerfully because these are the paths of their own loves.

On hearing this, all the members of the first group admitted that they too had thought about heaven strictly as a place where they would drink in overflowing joy with wide-open mouths.

The angel with the trumpet then said to them, "Now you see that heavenly joy and eternal happiness are not a matter of where you are but of the state of your life. The state of your life comes from your love and wisdom; and since service is the vessel of love and wisdom, a heavenly state of life comes from their union in service. We could just as well speak of charity, faith, and good works, since charity is love, faith is the truth that gives us wisdom, and good works are service to others.

"To be sure, there are places in our spiritual world just as there are in the earthly world. Otherwise there would be no homes, no separate houses. However, the nature of a place here is not physical. It is where something appears to be, based on our states of love and wisdom, or charity and faith.

"All the people who become angels bring their own heavens within themselves, because they bring a love of their own heaven. By creation, that is, we are miniature reflections, images, and models of the full-scale heaven. The human form is this and nothing else. This means that each of us winds up in the community of which each of us is a particular image; as a result, entering that community is entering something that corresponds to our own form. . . . We receive the life of the community as our own, and our own life as that of the community. Every community is a kind of inclusive body, and its angels are like the compatible parts from which the inclusive body arises in its totality."

Getting Around in Heaven

THERE ARE THREE HEAVENS

THERE ARE THREE HEAVENS, very clearly distinguished from each other. There is a central or third heaven, an intermediate or second one, and an outmost or first. These follow in sequence and are interdependent, like the highest part of the human body, the head; the middle, or torso; and the lowest, or feet; or like the highest, middle, and lowest parts of a house. The divine life that emanates and comes down from the Lord is in this kind of pattern as well. It is this necessity of design that determines the tripartite arrangement of heaven.

The deeper levels of the human mind and disposition are in a similar pattern as well. We have a central, intermediate, and outmost nature. This is because when humanity was created the whole divine design was gathered into it, to the point that as to structure, the human being is the divine design and is therefore a heaven in miniature. For the same reason we are in touch with heaven as to our inner natures and come into the company of angels after death—of angels of the central or the intermediate or the outmost heaven depending on our acceptance of divine good and truth from the Lord during our earthly lives.

The divine nature that flows from the Lord and is accepted in the third or central heaven is called heavenly, and the angels there are consequently called heavenly angels. The divine nature that flows from the Lord and is accepted in the second or intermediate heaven is called spiritual, and the angels there are consequently called spiritual angels. The divine nature, though, that flows from the Lord and is accepted in the outmost or first heaven is called natural. However, since the "natural" of that heaven is not like the "natural" of our world, but has something spiritual and heavenly within it, that heaven is called "spiritual-natural" or "heavenly-natural," and the angels there are called "spiritual-natural" or "heavenly-natural." The angels called spiritual-natural are the ones who accept an inflow from the intermediate or second heaven, which is the spiritual heaven, while the angels called heavenly-natural are the ones who accept an inflow from the central or third heaven, which is the heavenly heaven. Spiritual-natural and heavenly-natural angels are different from each other, but they constitute one heaven because they are all on the same level.

There is an outside and an inside to each heaven. The angels who are in the inner region are there called "inner angels," while the ones in the outer region are called "outer angels." The outside and the inside in the heavens (or in each particular heaven) are like our own volitional side and its cognitive aspect. Everything volitional has its cognitive side—neither occurs without the other. The volitional is like a flame and the cognitive like the light that it sheds.

It needs to be quite clear that it is the inner nature of angels that determines which heaven they are in. The more the deeper levels have been opened, the more inward the heaven they are in. There are three inner levels of every angel and spirit, and of every person here as well. The people whose third level has been opened are in the central heaven, while the people whose second or first only has been opened are in the intermediate or the outmost heaven.

The deeper levels are opened by our acceptance of divine good and divine true gifts. People who are actually affected by divine true gifts and let them directly into their lives—into their intentions and therefore into act—are in the central or third heaven, located there according to their acceptance of what is good in response to truth. People who do not let such gifts directly into their intentions, but into their memory and from there into their discernment, intending and doing them as a result of this process, are in the intermediate or second heaven. People who live good moral lives, though, and believe in the Divine with no particular interest in learning, are in the outmost or first heaven. We may therefore conclude that the state of our inner natures is what constitutes heaven and that heaven is within each one of us, not outside us. This is what the Lord teaches in saying, "The kingdom of God does not arrive when we are looking for it, nor do they say, 'Here it is,' or 'There it is.' Behold, you have the kingdom of God within you" (Luke 17:20–21).

All perfection increases as we move inward and decreases as we move outward, because more inward things are closer to the Lord and intrinsically purer, while more outward things are more remote from the Lord and intrinsically cruder. Angelic perfection consists of intelligence, wisdom, love, and everything good, with happiness as their result. It does not consist in happiness without these former qualities, since happiness without them is merely superficial, with no depth.

Since the inner reaches of angels of the central heaven are opened at the third level, their perfection far surpasses that of angels in the intermediate heaven, whose inner reaches are opened at the second level. By the same token, the perfection of angels of the intermediate heaven surpasses that of angels of the outmost heaven.

Because of this difference, an angel of one heaven cannot gain admission to angels of another heaven: someone from a lower heaven cannot come up, nor can someone from a higher heaven come down. Anyone who comes up is seized by anxiety even to the point of pain and cannot see the people who are there, let alone talk with them. Anyone who comes down from a higher heaven loses his or her wisdom, stammers, and loses confidence....

We can see from all this that the three heavens are quite distinct from each other. However, people who live in the same heaven can associate with anyone there, and their delight in getting together is in proportion to the similarity of the values they are devoted to.

Even though the heavens are so distinct from each other that angels of one heaven cannot have regular dealings with angels of another, still the Lord unites all the heavens by means of a direct and an indirect inflow. The direct inflow is from him into all the heavens, and the indirect is through one heaven into another. In this way, the Lord brings about a unity of the three heavens. They are all linked together, from the First to the last, so that nothing exists that is not connected. Anything that is not connected to the First by some intermediary does not endure, but disintegrates and becomes nothing.

Anyone who does not know how the divine design is arranged in levels cannot grasp how the heavens are distinguished from each other, or for that matter, what the inner person and the outer person are (in an individual). The only idea most people in this world have about inner and outer things is one of continuity, or of a coherence along a continuum from the finer to the coarser. Inner and outer things are not arranged in a continuum, though, but with definite boundaries.

There are two kinds of levels, continuous and noncontinuous. Continuous levels are like decreasing levels of light from a flame, all the way to darkness, or like decreasing amounts of sight from objects in the light to objects in the shade, or like levels of density of the atmosphere from the lowest to the highest. These levels are measured by distance.

Noncontinuous or distinct levels, though, are separated like prior and posterior, cause and effect, producer and product. Anyone who looks closely will discover that there are these kinds of stages of production and composition in everything in the world, no matter what, with one thing arising from another, and a third from that, and so forth.

People who do not acquire a grasp of these levels have no way of knowing how the heavens are arranged or the arrangement of our own deeper and more outward abilities, or the difference between the spiritual world and the natural world, or the difference between our spirit and our body. This also means they cannot understand what correspondences and images are or what inflow is like. People who are attentive only to their physical senses do not grasp these differences, but regard them as instances of increase and decrease on the model of continuous levels. As a result, they cannot think of the spiritual except as a kind of purer natural; so they stand outside, far removed from intelligence.

Lastly, let me disclose a particular secret about the angels of the three heavens that people have not been aware of until now because they have not understood levels. It is this, that within every angel—and within every one of us here—there is a central or highest level, or a central and highest something, where the Lord's divine life flows in first and most intimately. It is from this center that the Lord arranges the other, relatively internal aspects within us that follow in sequence according to the levels of the overall design. This central or highest level can be called the Lord's gateway to the angels or to us, his essential dwelling within us.

It is this central or highest level that makes us human and distinguishes us from the lower animals, since they do not have it. This is why we, unlike animals, can be raised up by the Lord toward himself, as far as all the deeper levels of our mind and character are concerned. This is why we can believe in him, be moved by love for him, and therefore see him. It is why we can receive intelligence and wisdom, and talk rationally. It is also why we live forever.

However, what is arranged and provided by the Lord at this center does not flow into the open perception of any angel, because it is higher than angelic thought, and surpasses angelic wisdom.

SPACE IN HEAVEN

EVEN THOUGH EVERYTHING in heaven appears to be located in space just like things in our world, still angels have no notion or concept of location and space. Since this can only seem like a paradox, and since it is highly significant, I should like to shed some light on it.

All motion in the spiritual world is the effect of changes of inner states, to the point that motion is nothing but change of state. This is how I have been led by the Lord into the heavens and also to other planets in the universe. This happened to my spirit, while my body remained in the same place. This is how all angels move about, which means they do not have distances; and if they do not have distances, they do not have space. Instead they have states and their changes.

This being the nature of motion, we can see that drawing near is likeness of inner state and moving away is dissimilarity. This is why the people who are nearby are the ones in a similar state and the ones who are far away are in dissimilar states. It is why space in heaven is nothing but the outward states that correspond to the inner ones.

This is the only reason the heavens are differentiated from each other, as are the communities of each heaven and the individuals in each community. It is also why the hells are completely separate from the heavens: they are in an opposite state.

This is also why in the spiritual world one individual is present to another if only that presence is intensely desired. This is because one person sees another in thought in this way and identifies with that individual's state. Conversely, one person moves away from another to the extent that there is any sense of reluctance; and since all reluctance comes from an opposition of affections and disagreement of thoughts, there can be many people appearing together in one place as long as they agree, but as soon as they disagree, they vanish.

Whenever people move from one place to another, whether it is within their town, in their courtyards, in their gardens, or to people outside their own community, they get there more quickly if they are eager to and more slowly if they are not. The path itself is lengthened or shortened depending on their desire, even though it is the same path. I have often seen this, much to my surprise.

We can see from all this again that distance and space itself depend wholly on the inner state of angels; and since this is the case, no notion or concept of space can enter their minds even though they have space just the way we do in our world.

We can illustrate this by our own thoughts, which are also devoid of space; for whatever we focus on intently in our thought is seemingly present. Then too, anyone who reflects on it realizes that our eyesight registers space only through the intermediate objects on earth that we see at the same time, or from our knowing from experience that things are a certain distance away. This is because we are dealing with a continuum, and in a continuum there is no apparent distance except by means of discontinuities. This is even more the case for angels because their sight acts in unison with their thought, and their thought in unison with their affection, and also because things seem near or remote, and things change, in response to the states of their deeper natures, as already noted. . . .

We can see from this that even though there is space in heaven as there is in our world, nothing there is evaluated on the basis of space, but only on the basis of state. Also spaces there cannot be measured the way they can in our world, but only seen out of and in accordance with the state of their deeper natures.

The essential first cause of all this is that the Lord is present to each individual according to that individual's love and faith, and that everything looks near or remote depending on his presence, since this is what defines everything that exists in the heavens. This is what gives angels wisdom, since it provides them with an outreach of thoughts, which in turn affords them communication with everyone in the heavens. In a word, this is what enables them to think spiritually and not naturally, the way we do.

TIME IN HEAVEN

EVEN THOUGH THINGS keep happening in sequence and progressing in heaven the way they do in the world, still angels have no notion or concept of time and space. The lack is so complete that they simply do not know what time and space are. Here we will discuss time in heaven.

The reason angels do not know what time is (even though everything for them moves along in sequence just the way it does in our world, so much so that there is no difference) is that in heaven there are no years or days, but only changes of state. Where there are years and days there are times, and where there are changes of state, there are states.

The reason we have times in our world is that the sun seems to move sequentially from one zone to another and to make the times we call the seasons of the year. It also moves around the earth and makes the times we call times of day, and it does these by fixed periods.

It is different for heaven's sun. It does not make years and days by sequential motions and rotations, but makes apparent changes of state; and it does not make these by fixed periods. This is why angels are incapable of having any concept of time, but have a concept of state instead.

Since angels have no concept derived from time, as we in our world do, they have no concept of time or of the things that depend on time. They do not even know what all these temporal things are, like a year, a month, a week, a day, an hour, today, tomorrow, or yesterday. When angels hear these expressions from one of us (angels are always kept in contact with us by the Lord), they perceive states instead, and things that have to do with state. So our natural concept is changed into a spiritual concept with the angels. This is why expressions of time in the Word mean states, and why things proper to time like the ones listed above mean the spiritual things that correspond to them.

It is much the same for all the things that occur as a result of time, such as the four seasons of the year called spring, summer, autumn, and winter; the four times of day called morning, noon, evening, and night; our own four ages called infancy, youth, maturity, and old age; and with the other things that either occur as a result of time or happen in temporal sequence. When we think about them, it is from a temporal standpoint; but an angel thinks about them from the standpoint of state. Consequently, anything in them that is temporal for us changes into an idea of state for the angel. Spring and morning change into an idea of love and wisdom the way they are for angels in their first state; summer and noon change into an idea of love and wisdom as they are in the second state; autumn and evening, as they are in the third state; and night and winter into a concept of the kind of state that is characteristic in hell. This is why similar things are meant by these times in the

Word. We can see from this how the natural concepts that occur in our thought become spiritual for the angels who are with us.

Since angels have no notion of time, they have a different concept of eternity than we earthly people do. By "eternity," angels perceive an infinite state, not an infinite time.

I was thinking about eternity once, and using a concept of time I could grasp what "to eternity" entailed—namely, without end—but not what "from eternity" entailed and therefore not what God did before creation, from eternity. As my anxiety mounted because of this, I was raised into the sphere of heaven and therefore into the perception of eternity shared by angels. This shed light for me on the fact that we ought not to think about eternity in temporal terms but in terms of state, and that when we do, we can grasp what "from eternity" entails, which was actually done for me.

The angels who talk with us never use the natural concepts that are proper to us, all of which derive from time, space, matter, and the like. They use spiritual concepts, all of which derive from states and their various changes in and around angels. However, when the angelic concepts, which are spiritual, flow into us, they change instantly and spontaneously into those natural concepts proper to us which exactly correspond to the spiritual ones. Neither the angels nor we are aware of this; but still, this is how all inflow of heaven occurs for us.

There were some angels who were let very intimately into my thoughts, all the way into natural ones that contained a mass of material from time and space. However, since at that point they could not understand anything at all, they promptly withdrew; and after they had withdrawn I heard them talking, saying that they had been in darkness.

I have been allowed to know from experience what angels' ignorance of time is like. There was a particular individual from heaven whose nature did allow him to be let into natural concepts such as we have. I talked with him afterward, person to person, and at first he did not know what it was that I was calling "time." So I actually had to tell him how the sun seems to travel around our earth and make years and days, and that as a result, years are divided into four seasons and into months and weeks, and days into twenty-four hours, and that these times recur at fixed intervals. This gives rise to our expressions for time. He was astonished when he heard this, and said that he had not known that kind of thing, but only what states were.

In the course of our conversation I mentioned that it was known in our world that there is no time in heaven. We do actually talk as though we knew, since when people die, we say that they have left temporal things and have passed beyond time, meaning that they have left our world. I also said that it is known by some that times are states in origin because they recognize that times are experienced in precise accord with the states of affection we are caught up in. They are short for us when we are engaged in pleasant and cheerful pursuits and long when we are engaged in distasteful and depressing ones, and variable when we are in hope or expectation. As a result, scholars are asking what time and space are, and some of them even recognize that time is an attribute of the natural person.

A natural person may believe that we would have no thought if concepts of time, space, and matter were taken away from us, that all our thought is based on these foundations. Let such people know, though, that thoughts are limited and constrained to the extent that they derive from time, space, and matter, and that they are freed and expanded to the extent that they do not derive from such things, because to that same extent the mind is raised above bodily and worldly considerations. This is the source of angels' wisdom, which is so great that we must call it incomprehensible, since it does not fit into ideas that are formed merely from these [lower] concerns.

Daily Life

COMMUNITIES IN HEAVEN

THE ANGELS OF ANY GIVEN HEAVEN are not all together in one place, but are separated into larger and smaller communities depending on differences in the good effects of the love and faith they are engaged in. Angels engaged in similar activities form a single community. There is an infinite variety of good activities in heaven, and each individual angel is, so to speak, his or her own activity.

The distances between angelic communities in the heavens also vary as their activities vary, in general and in detail. This is because the only cause of distance in the spiritual world is the difference of the state of our more inward natures—in the heavens, then, differences in the state of love. When communities are very different, the distance between them is great; when the difference is slight, the distance is slight. Likeness makes for unity.

All the individuals in a single community are distanced from each other by the same principle. The better ones, that is, the ones who are more complete in goodness and therefore in love, wisdom, and intelligence, are in the center. Those who are less outstanding surround them at distances graded in proportion to their lessened perfection. It is like the way light decreases from a center toward a circumference. The ones who are in the middle are in the greatest light, while the ones who are toward the perimeter are in less and less.

Kindred souls gravitate toward each other spontaneously, as it were, for with each other they feel as though they are with their own family, at home, while with others they feel like foreigners, as though they were abroad. When they are with kindred souls, they enjoy the fullest freedom and find life totally delightful.

We can see from this that the good gathers everyone together in the heavens, and that angels are differentiated by what good they do. Still, it is not the angels who gather themselves, but the Lord, the source of all that is good. He leads them, unites them, differentiates them, and keeps them in freedom to the extent that they are engaged in what is good. So he keeps every individual in the life of his or her own love, faith, intelligence, and wisdom— and therefore in happiness.

Further, people of similar quality all recognize each other there just the way people in this world recognize their neighbors and relatives and friends, even though they may never have seen each other before. This happens because the only relationships and kinships and friendships in the other life are spiritual ones, and are therefore matters of love and faith.

I have often been allowed to see this when I was in the spirit and therefore out of body and in the company of angels. Then some of them looked to me as though I had known them from infancy, while others seemed totally unfamiliar. The ones who looked as though I had known them from infancy were the ones who were in a state like that of my own spirit, while the unfamiliar ones were in dissimilar states.

All the individuals who make up a particular angelic community have a general facial resemblance, but differ in detail. I could grasp this general similarity and particular difference to some extent on the basis of similar situations in this world. We know that every race has a general similarity about the face and eyes that enables us to recognize it and distinguish it from other races, and that the same is even more true from one family to another. This holds true much more perfectly in the heavens, because there all the deeper feelings are visible and shine forth from the face, the face there being their outward and graphic form. It is not possible in heaven to have a face that differs from our feelings.

I have also been shown how this general similarity is varied in detail in the individuals of a single community. There was a kind of angelic face that appeared to me, and this was varied according to the qualities of affections for the good and the true that were characteristic of the individuals in a particular community. These variations lasted quite a while, and through it all I noticed that the same general face remained constant as a basis, with everything else being simply derivations and elaborations from it. In this way, too, I was shown the affections of the whole community that occasioned the differences in the faces of its members, for as already noted, the faces of angels are their deeper qualities taking form, which means they are forms of the affections proper to their love and faith.

This is also why an angel of outstanding wisdom sees the quality of others instantly, from their faces. In heaven, no one can conceal inner character by facial expression and pretend, much less lie and deceive others by guile and hypocrisy.

It does sometimes happen that hypocrites steal into [heavenly] communities, hypocrites trained in hiding their inner nature and arranging their outward appearance in the benevolent form they present in public, thereby misleading angels of light. However, they cannot stay around very long. They begin to feel inner discomfort and torment, their faces start to turn blue, and they almost faint—changes caused by their opposition to the life that is flowing in and affecting them. So they promptly cast themselves back into the hell of people like themselves and no longer dare to climb up again. These are the people meant by the man who was discovered among the dinner guests without a wedding garment and was thrown out into outer darkness (Matthew 22:11[–14]).

All the communities communicate with each other, but not through open interaction. Actually, not many individuals leave their own community to go to another, because leaving their community is like leaving themselves or their life and crossing over into another that does not suit them. Rather, they all communicate by the outreach of the auras that emanate from the life of every individual. An aura of life is an aura of affections based in love and faith. This reaches out far and wide into surrounding communities, farther and wider as the affections are deeper and more perfect. Angels possess intelligence and wisdom in proportion to this outreach. The ones who are in the most inward heaven and therefore at the center have an outreach into all of heaven, so that there is a communication of everyone in heaven with each individual and of each individual with everyone.

We have noted above that there are larger and smaller communities in the heavens. The larger ones consist of tens of thousands of individuals, the smaller of some thousands, and the smallest of hundreds. There are even people who live alone, house by house, so to speak, and family by family. Even though they live apart, they are still arranged in the same pattern as those who live in communities, with the wiser of them in the center and the simpler at the periphery. They are very closely under the Lord's guidance, and are the best of angels.

ANGELS' HOMES

SINCE THERE ARE COMMUNITIES in heaven, with people living there the way we do, they too have homes; and these vary depending on the state of the life of each individual. They are splendid for people who are especially deserving and less splendid for people who are of lower rank. . . .

Whenever I have talked with angels face to face, I have been with them in their houses. Their houses were just like the houses on earth that we call homes, but more beautiful. They have chambers, suites, and bedrooms in abundance, and courtyards with gardens, flower beds, and lawns around them. Where there is some concentration of people, the houses are adjoining, one near another, arranged in the form of a city with streets and lanes and public squares, just like the ones we see in cities on our earth. I have been allowed to stroll along them and look around wherever I wished, at times entering people's homes. This has happened when I was fully awake, with my inner sight opened.

I have seen palaces in heaven that were so splendid as to be beyond description. Their upper stories shone as though they were made of pure gold, and their lower ones as though they were made of precious gems. Each palace seemed more splendid than the last. It was the same inside. The rooms were graced with such lovely adornments that neither words nor the arts and sciences are adequate to describe them. On the side that faced south there were parklands where everything sparkled in the same way, here and there the leaves like silver and the fruits like gold, with the flowers in their beds making virtual rainbows with their colors. On the horizon of sight there were other palaces that framed the scene. The architecture of heaven is like this, so that you might call it the very essence of the art—and small wonder, since the art itself does come to us from heaven. . . .

The angels who constitute the Lord's heavenly kingdom live for the most part in loftier places that look like mountains above the ground. The angels who constitute the Lord's spiritual kingdom live in less lofty places that look like hills, while the angels who live in the lowest regions of heaven live in places that look like rocky cliffs. These things also stem from correspondences, since the deeper things correspond to higher ones and the more outward to lower ones. This is why mountains in the Word mean heavenly love, hills mean spiritual love, and rocks mean faith. . . .

The houses angels live in are not constructed as houses in our world are, but are given them by the Lord gratis, to each individual according to his or her acceptance of what is good and true. They also change slightly in response to the changes of state of their deeper natures.

Whatever angels possess, they attribute to the Lord, and anything they need is given to them.

AMAZING SIGHTS IN HEAVEN

AMAZING SIGHTS CAN BE SEEN by the Lord's light in heaven—so many of them that they could never be listed. These sights consist of one scene after another representing the Lord and his kingdom, resembling scenes described by the prophets and by John in the book of Revelation. There are other symbolic objects as well. We cannot possibly see them with our physical eyes, but as soon as the Lord opens our inner eyes—the eyes of our spirit—similar sights can immediately present themselves to view. The visions of the prophets were nothing more than the opening of their inner eyes. This is what happened when John saw the golden lampstands (Revelation 1:12, 13), the holy city as pure gold, and its light source like a very precious stone (Revelation 21:2, 10, [11, 18]), not to mention much in the prophets. These considerations teach not only that angels live in the highest light but also that heaven contains countless marvels that no one could ever believe.

Until my eyes were opened, I almost inevitably cherished the same idea as others about the countless wonders that appear in the next world. I thought that neither light nor the kind of phenomena light creates—to say nothing of sensory powers—could possibly exist in the next world. This thinking grew out of a delusion that the well-educated adopt concerning immateriality, which they ascribe so broadly to spirits and to everything in a spirit's life. Such a delusion could yield only one way to conceive of anything spiritual: that because it lacked matter, either it was too vague to be grasped in any way or it was nothing at all. That is what "immaterial" means, of course. The reality is diametrically opposed. If spirits were not organic—and if angels were not organic substances—they would not be able to speak or see or think. . . .

There are more objects to be seen in the world of spirits and heaven than can be listed. As the present subject is light, let me tell about the things that arise directly out of the light, such as atmospheres, parks, rainbows, palaces, and houses. With their outward eyes, spirits and angels see these items as being so radiant and alive, so perceptible to all their senses, that they declare them to be real and the objects of the world to be unreal by comparison.

I start with the atmospheres that the blessed live in, which are made of light, because they rise out of the light there. The number of different kinds cannot be counted, and they are so beautiful and pleasant that they cannot be described. There are diamond-like atmospheres that flash in all their most minuscule elements, as if they were made of diamond pellets. There are atmospheres that resemble the gleam of all kinds of gems. There are atmospheres seemingly made of translucent pearls glowing from within, streaking the air with the most brilliant colors. There are atmospheres afire with gold, it seems, or with silver, or with diamond-like gold and silver. There are atmospheres composed of multicolored flowers so small they cannot be seen; countless variations on this type of atmosphere fill the heaven where small children live. In fact one even sees atmospheres composed of what seem to be children at play, again at a size that is too small to see but that can be perceived, although only by the deepest power of thought. This gives young children the idea that everything around them is alive and is part of the Lord's stream of life—a thought that gladdens them to the core.

There are many other kinds of atmosphere besides, because the variations are beyond number and also beyond description.

To turn now to the magnificent gardens: they are breathtaking. Huge parks containing every kind of tree come into view, so beautiful and so charming that they defy all power of imagination. They are presented to the inhabitants' outward sight in such a living way that not only are they seen, they are also perceived in all their detail much more vividly than anything our physical eyesight discerns on earth.

To remove any doubts I might have on the subject, I was taken there (where people who live the life of paradise are located), and I saw. Absolutely everything appears in its loveliest springtime and its loveliest bloom, with stunning magnificence and variety. Every single object is alive with representation, since nothing exists there that does not represent or symbolize something heavenly or spiritual. So the sights not only please the eyes but also cheer the mind. . . .

As for rainbows, there is a kind of iridescent heaven, in which the whole atmosphere seems to be made of tiny rainbows, one after another. The entire atmosphere there—all the air—consists of these gleams of light and therefore radiates out of each individual "beacon," so to speak.

A much larger rainbow (compounded of similar smaller ones that are exquisite miniatures of the big one) forms a gorgeous belt around the outside.

Each color, then, consists of many, many rays, so that millions of rays make up a single, all-inclusive rainbow visible to the eye. The rainbow is a modification of the points of light, a modification produced by the heavenly and spiritual forces that create the rainbow and in the process present before the observer's eyes a picture full of representative meaning.

There is no limit to the different types and varieties of rainbows, several of which I was privileged to see. To grasp in some measure the kind of variation they display, and to see how very many rays of light go into a single visible one, let me describe just one or two.

Once a large-scale rainbow appeared before me so that I could learn from it what rainbows are like at the smallest scale. There was a brilliant white light with a kind of belt about it. At the core of the belt was something dim and earthlike surrounded by a bright radiance. The radiance was dappled and broken up by another kind of light containing golden star-like sparkles. Other changes occurred when flowers of different colors entered into the bright radiance—colors produced not by white light but by a fiery kind of light. All of it represented heavenly and spiritual qualities.

In the other world, all visible colors represent something heavenly or spiritual. Colors that partake of fire represent aspects of love and of a desire for what is good. Colors that partake of white light represent aspects of faith and of a desire for truth. All colors in the next life come from these sources and therefore gleam so brilliantly that colors in this world cannot be compared to them. There are also colors that have never been seen in the world.

A rainbow shape with something grass-like and green at its center also appeared, and I sensed a kind of sun off to the side, out of sight, gleaming, and giving off a light so bright that it cannot be described. At the edges were the most beautiful variations of color possible, in a luminescent, pearly field.

These and other experiences showed me what a rainbow is like in its smallest components. They also showed me that there is no end to the number of variations, which depend on neighborly love and the resulting faith in an individual who sees them represented. That individual in turn looks like a rainbow to others when presented to their view in all her or his beauty and glory.

In addition to these wonders of paradise, one also sees cities full of splendid mansions, one after another, gleaming with color, beyond the skill of any architect to create. Not surprisingly, cities like them appeared to the prophets as well, when their inner eyes were open; and these cities were as plain to see as any that could exist in the world. The New Jerusalem appeared to John, for instance, and he described it in these words:

> He took me away *in spirit* onto a mountain big and high and showed me the great city, Jerusalem the Holy, having a wall big and high, having twelve gates. The structure of the wall was jasper, and the city was pure gold, like golden glass. The foundations of the wall were adorned with every precious stone. The first foundation was jasper, the second sapphire,

the third chalcedony, the fourth emerald, the fifth sardonyx, the sixth sard, the seventh chrysolite, the eighth beryl, the ninth topaz, the tenth chrysoprase, the eleventh hyacinth, the twelfth amethyst. (Revelation 21:10, 12, 18, 19, 20)

The prophets also describe the new Jerusalem.

Sights like these in countless numbers appear to angels and angelic spirits in broad daylight, and surprising to say, the angels and spirits perceive them with all their senses. This will never be believed by anyone who has blotted out all spiritual thinking by means of the terms and definitions used in human philosophy and by argumentation—yet it is absolutely true. The fact that the saints saw them so many times could have convinced such people that it is true.

In addition to cities and mansions, I was sometimes able to see decorative elements, such as those that appear on stairways and main doors. These elements moved as if they were alive, and changed with ever fresh beauty and symmetry. I learned that such changes can keep going indefinitely, one after another, even to eternity, and there is a constantly renewed harmony among the variations, formed by the very sequence of changes itself. These were only the least of their wonders, I heard.

All angels have their own houses to live in—magnificent houses. While there, I saw them several times, with astonishment, and spoke with the angels in them. They are so clear to see, so visible, that nothing could be more so. Houses on earth are almost nothing by comparison. Angels also call earthly dwellings lifeless and unreal but their own dwellings alive and genuine, because they come from the Lord. The architecture is such that it is the source of the art itself, with unending variety.

They said that if they were given all the palaces in the whole inhabited world, they would not exchange their own for them. Anything made of stone, brick, or plank seems dead to them, but anything from the Lord, or from life and light itself, is alive. Such materials are all the more alive because angels experience them with the full range of senses, since objects there are perfectly suited to the senses of spirits and angels. Objects in the light of the sun's realm are not the least bit visible to spirits' eyes. To the senses we have in our bodies, though, stone and wood are well-suited. What is spiritual responds to what is spiritual, and what is physical responds to what is physical.

The houses of good spirits and angelic spirits usually have porticoes, or long entryways, vaulted and sometimes doubled, where they walk. The walls of the walkways are formed in many different ways and are graced with flowers and flower garlands woven in an extraordinary manner, not to mention other kinds of decoration that change and replace one another, as noted. These details appear to them in brighter light at one time, in weaker light at another, but always offering profound pleasure.

Their houses also turn more beautiful as the spirits grow in perfection. When the houses are undergoing change, something representing a window appears at the side and widens, and the inside grows darker. A piece of starry sky appears, as does a kind of cloud, which is a sign that their houses are changing into even more enchanting ones.

Spirits are quite disgusted by the poor opinion people have of the life that spirits and angels enjoy. They are upset to know that we imagine them as existing in a dim, obscure state (which would have to be awfully grim) and inhabiting a kind of vacuum or void.

The truth is that they have the greatest possible light, enjoy every benefit available to each of the senses, and feel it very deeply.

There were also some souls just come from the world who brought with them (from assumptions they had adopted there) the idea that such vitality was not possible in the other world. As a result, they were taken into angel homes, where they talked with the angels and saw what was there. When they returned, they kept saying, "I can see it's true!" "Those things are real!" "I would never have believed this during life in the body. I never *could* have." They said that these have to be some of the most amazing things that exist, but no one believes in such things because no one understands them. Just because they do not understand it—and this is something they are told—they should not doubt it, since it is a matter to be experienced by the senses (the inner senses, at any rate). After all, if we believed only what we could grasp, we would not believe in anything at the microscopic level of the physical world, let alone anything having to do with eternal life.

That is what produces the insanity of our era. . . .

With angels I have discussed representations and the fact that nothing in the plant kingdom on earth fails to represent the Lord's kingdom in some way. They have said that every pretty and attractive specimen of the plant kingdom comes from the Lord by way of heaven; and since the Lord's heavenly and spiritual forces act on the physical world, they actually take on a visible form. That is where the soul or life of plants comes from, and it is the reason that they represent something. As this is unknown in the world, it is called a heavenly secret.

ANGELS' CLOTHING

SINCE ANGELS ARE PEOPLE and live together the way people on earth do, they have clothes and homes and a great many other things: the difference, however, being that everything is more perfect for them because they are in a more perfect state. For just as angelic wisdom surpasses our wisdom so greatly as to be inexpressible, so too does everything that comes to their perception and sight, since everything perceived by and apparent to angels corresponds to their wisdom.

Like everything else, the clothes angels wear correspond [to their inner state], and since they do correspond they truly exist. Their clothes reflect their intelligence, so all the people in heaven are dressed according to their intelligence; and since one will surpass another in intelligence, one will have better quality clothing than another. The most intelligent wear clothes that gleam as though aflame, some radiant as though alight. The less intelligent wear pure white and soft white clothes that do not shine, and those still less intelligent wear clothes of various colors. The angels of the inmost heaven, though, are naked.

Because angels' clothes correspond to their intelligence they also correspond to what is true, since all intelligence comes from divine truth. So it amounts to the same thing whether you say that angels are dressed according to their intelligence or according to divine truth. The reason the garments of some angels gleam as though aflame, while the garments of others shine as though alight, is that flame corresponds to what is good, and light to what is true because of that good. The reason some garments are pure white and soft white and do not shine, while others are of various colors, is that divine good and truth are less dazzling and are also differently accepted among less intelligent people. Pure white and soft white correspond to what is true, and colors correspond to different shadings of truth. The reason angels in the inmost heaven are naked is that they are in innocence, and innocence corresponds to nudity. . . .

We can tell that angels' clothes do not merely look like clothes but really are because they not only see them, they feel them as well. Further, they have many garments that they take off and put on, and they put away the ones they are not using and put back on the ones they are. I have seen thousands of times that they wear different clothes.

I have asked them where they got their clothes, and they have told me that their clothes come from the Lord and are given to them, and that sometimes they are clothed without noticing it. They have also said that their clothes change depending on the changes of their state, that their clothes are radiant and gleaming white in their first and second state, while in the third and fourth states they are somewhat dimmer. This too is because of correspondences, because these changes of state have to do with their intelligence and wisdom.

For everyone in the spiritual world, clothing depends on intelligence and therefore on the truths that constitute intelligence. Although people in the hells do seem to be clothed, because they lack truths their clothes are nothing but rags, dirty and foul, each individual in keeping with his or her own insanity. They cannot be clothed in any other way, either. The Lord allows them to wear clothes so that they will not appear naked.

WHAT ANGELS DO

THERE IS NO WAY TO LIST all the functions that people have in the heavens or to describe them in detail, though it is possible to say something on the subject in general terms; they are innumerable and vary depending on the roles of the communities as well. In fact, each community plays a unique role, since the communities differ depending on their virtues and therefore on their function. This is because virtues for everyone in the heavens are virtues in act, which are functions. Everyone there does something specifically useful, for the Lord's kingdom is a kingdom of uses. . . .

Everything in the heavens is arranged according to the divine design, which is managed everywhere by the oversight of angels, with the wiser ones tending to matters of the common good or use and the less wise to smaller details, and so on. These matters are ranked just as uses are ranked in the divine design. This also means that importance is attributed to each role in keeping with the importance of its use. Angels, however, do not claim any importance for themselves but ascribe it all to the use; and since the use is the good that it serves and everything good comes from the Lord, they ascribe it all to the Lord. This means that if people think about respect for themselves first and for their use secondarily instead of for the use first and for themselves secondarily, they cannot hold any office in heaven because they are looking away from the Lord, putting themselves first and their use second. To say "use" is to mean the Lord as well, since as just noted use is something good, and good comes from the Lord.

This enables us to determine what rankings in the heavens are like, namely that we love, value, and respect the functionaries the way we love, value, and respect the functions that are associated with them, and also that these functionaries are loved, valued, and respected to the extent that they do not attribute their use to themselves but to the Lord. To that extent they are wise, and to that extent they fulfill their uses from good motives. Spiritual love, value, and respect are nothing but love, value, and respect for the use in the role, respect for the role because of the use and not for the use because of the role. If we look at people from a spiritually true perspective, this is the only way to see them. Then we see one person as much like another, whether their rank is great or small. The only difference we see is a difference in wisdom, and wisdom is loving use, which means loving the welfare of our fellow citizens, our community, our country, and the church.

This is also what constitutes love for the Lord, since everything good that is effectively good comes from the Lord. It also constitutes love for our neighbor, since our neighbor is the welfare that is to be loved in our fellow citizens, our community, our country, and our church, and that is to be fostered for their sakes.

All the communities in the heavens are differentiated according to their forms of service because they are differentiated according to their virtues. Their virtues are virtues in action or acts of thoughtfulness, which are services. There are some communities whose tasks are to take care of babies; there are other communities whose tasks are to teach and lead children while they are growing up; there are other communities that look after young boys and girls who are well disposed because of the way they were raised in this world and have come [straight] to heaven, where they are taught and raised in much the same way. There are some that teach simple people from the Christian world and lead them on the way to heaven, and there are some that do the same for various non-Christian peoples. There are some that protect new spirits, just arrived from the world, from the attacks of evil spirits; and there are some who attend to people in the lower earth. Then there are some who attend to people in the hells and control them so that they do not torture each other beyond set limits. There are also some who tend to people who are being awakened from their death.

Broadly speaking, angels of all communities are assigned to us to protect us, to lead us away from evil feelings and the evil thoughts that these cause and to instill good feelings to the extent that we are freely open to them. These serve to control our deeds or works by removing our evil intentions to the extent that this can be done. When angels are with us they seem to dwell in our affections, near us to the extent that we are engaged in something good because of truth, and distant to the extent that our life is removed from such engagement.

However, all these tasks are things the Lord does by means of angels, since angels do them not on their own but from the Lord. This is why in the deeper meaning of the Word "angels" does not mean angels but something of the Lord; and this is why angels are called gods in the Word.

These are general categories of angels' activities, but each individual has her or his own specific contribution to make. This is because every general service is made up of countless elements that are called mediate or subservient or supporting services. All of these are arranged and ranked according to the divine design, and taken together they make up and complete an overarching function that is the common good.

The people in heaven who are involved in church affairs are the ones who loved the Word in the world and looked for truths in it with lively interest, not for the sake of eminence or profit but for the service of their own life and the lives of others. In proportion to their love and eagerness for service, they are enlightened there and are in the light of wisdom, attaining it because of the Word in the heavens, which is not natural the way it is in the world, but spiritual. They have the gift of preaching; and in keeping with the divine design, the ones who are more highly placed there are the ones who surpass others in the wisdom they derive from their enlightenment.

The people who are involved in civic affairs are the ones who loved their country and its welfare more than their own, who behaved honestly and fairly out of a love for what is honest and fair. To the extent that they sought out laws of justice because of the urging of this love and thereby became discerning they enjoy the ability to fill governing offices in heaven. They perform these duties in the place or on the level appropriate to their discernment, which in turn is equivalent to their love of service in the common good.

Further, there are so many offices and departments in heaven, so many tasks, that there are simply too many to list. There are relatively few in the world. No matter how many people are involved, they are all caught up in a love of their work and tasks out of a love of service—no one out of selfishness or a love of profit. In fact, there is no love of profit for the sake of livelihood, since all the necessities of life are given them gratis. They are housed gratis, clothed gratis, and fed gratis. We can see from this that people who have loved themselves and the world more than service have no place in heaven. In fact, our love or affection invariably stays with us after our life in the world. It is not uprooted to eternity.

Everyone in heaven is engaged in his or her work according to its correspondence, and the correspondence is not with the work itself but with the use of each particular task. When we are engaged in an activity or a task in heaven that does answer to its use, then we are in a state of life very much like the one we were in in this world. This is because what is spiritual and what is natural act as one by means of their correspondence, but with the difference that [after death] we enjoy a deeper delight because we are engaged in a spiritual life. This is a deeper life, and therefore more open to heavenly blessedness.

Love and Marriage

MARRIED PARTNERS AFTER DEATH

[BECAUSE ELSEWHERE] I HAVE EXPLAINED that there are marriages in heaven, we come to the question of whether or not a marriage contract made in the world will continue in force after death. Since this is not a matter of arbitrary judgment but a matter of eyewitness experience, and since I have been granted this experience by my association with angels and spirits, I am under obligation to convey it, though in a way that enlists the support of reason as well.

One of the prayers and longings of married partners is to know this. Widowers who have loved their wives want to know whether their wives are doing well, and by the same token widows who have loved their husbands want to know whether they will meet again. Then too, many partners would like to know in advance whether they will be separated or will live together after death. If they have been at odds spiritually, they want to know whether they will be separated, and if they have been in harmony spiritually, they want to know whether they will live together. Because of the keen interest in this information, it is communicated here. . . .

After death, we all retain our love for the opposite sex as it was inwardly, that is, as it was within our intending and thinking in the world. All of our love stays with us after death because it is the very substance of our life; and the dominant love, the head of the others, stays with us to eternity along with its subordinate loves. The reason they last is that, strictly speaking, love is our spirit, and the body comes from the spirit. After death, we are spirits, so we bring our love with us; and since love is the very substance of our life, we can see that the nature of our life in the world determines what will become of us after death.

As for our love for the opposite sex, this is the most inclusive of all because at our creation it was instilled into our very soul, which is the source of our whole human nature, this for the sake of the propagation of the human race. The reason this love is particularly lasting is that after death a man is a man and a woman is a woman: there is nothing in our souls, our minds, or our bodies that is not masculine in the male and feminine in the female. These two natures have been so created as to strive toward union, and in fact toward such a complete union that they become one. This striving is love for the opposite sex, the precursor of the love of marriage.

Since the tendency to unite is engraved on every detail of the male and the female, then, it follows that this tendency cannot be erased or die when the body dies.

The reason our abiding love for the opposite sex retains the nature it had inwardly in this world is that there is an inner and an outer level to everyone, commonly referred to as an inner self and an outer self. This means that we have an inner and an outer intention and thought. When we die, we leave the outer behind but keep the inner. Strictly speaking, our outer concerns focus on our bodies and our inner concerns focus on our spirits.

Since each of us is our love, then, and since love dwells in our spirit, it follows that the love for the opposite sex that remains with us after death is our love as it was inwardly. So for example, if that love was inwardly intent upon marriage and was chaste, then it remains intent upon marriage and chaste after death. If on the other hand it was intent upon infidelity, it stays that way after death as well.

However, we need to realize that love for the opposite sex is not the same in one person as in another; its differences are infinite in number. Still, whatever it was like in our spirit, so it remains.

By the same token, our love of marriage remains as it was inwardly—that is, in our inner intending and thinking—while we were in the world. Since love for the opposite sex is not the same thing as the love of marriage, I am giving each a distinct name and saying that the latter, too, remains the same for us after death as it was inwardly, in our inner self, while we were living in the world. However, since not many people know the difference between love for the opposite sex and a love of marriage, as we enter this topic I need to make some introductory observations.

Love for the opposite sex is a love directed toward and shared with many members of the opposite sex, while the love of marriage is directed solely toward and shared with one member of the opposite sex. Love directed toward and shared with many is an earthly love that we have in common with beasts and birds, who are earthly; while the love of marriage is a spiritual love, uniquely and essentially human because we were created to become spiritual and are therefore born to become spiritual. As a result, to the extent that we do become spiritual we shed our general love for the opposite sex and adopt a love of marriage.

At the beginning of a marriage, love for the opposite sex seems inseparable from the love of marriage, but as the marriage progresses they part company. Then for people who are spiritual, that general love for the opposite sex is banished and a love of marriage is instilled, while with people who are earthly, the opposite happens.

This shows us that love for the opposite sex, since it is [directed toward and] shared with many and is intrinsically earthly, actually bestial, is impure and unchaste, and because it is wanton and uncontrolled, it is promiscuous; while the love of marriage is completely different.

In most cases, two partners will meet after death, recognize each other, and resume their relationship by living together for a while. This happens in their first state, when they are focused on external matters the way they were in the world. We undergo two states after death, one outer and one inner. We enter the outer one first and the inner one later. When they are in the outer state, after death one spouse meets the other and they recognize one another; and if they had been living together in the world [at the time the first of them died], they resume that relationship and live together for a while. As long as they are in the outer state, neither of them knows how the other truly feels about him or her because this is hidden within. Later, though, when they come into the inner state, the relationship between their hearts becomes obvious. If it is harmonious and sympathetic, they continue their married life; while if it is discordant and in conflict, they dissolve the relationship.

If a husband has had more than one wife, he lives with them in turn during the outer state; but once he enters the inner state, in which he senses the love that each of them has, then he chooses one or none of them. It is the same in the spiritual world as in this earthly world, that is: no Christian is allowed to have more than one wife because this offends and profanes his religion.

Much the same holds true for a woman who has had more than one husband, except that she does not initiate the attachment between her husband and herself; she simply makes herself present where her husband is. It is the husband who initiates the attachment.

It should be known that husbands rarely recognize their wives, but that wives recognize their husbands without difficulty. This is because women have a deeper sensitivity to love, while men's sensitivity to love is more superficial.

Gradually, though, as they leave these outward concerns behind and become involved in deeper matters, they sense the quality of their love for each other and attraction to each other, which determines whether or not they can live together.

After death, everyone is brought into a world called the world of spirits. It is halfway between heaven and hell and is where we are prepared for heaven if we are good and for hell if we are evil. The goal of this preparation is for our inner and outer selves to agree and be whole and not to disagree and be split in two. They are split in two in this world and are whole only in people who are honest at heart. The split is particularly obvious in perpetrators of deception and fraud, especially by hypocrites, sycophants, imposters, and liars.

In the spiritual world, however, no one is allowed to have this kind of divided mind. If we were inwardly evil, we must be outwardly evil as well, or, conversely, we must be good in both respects. After death, we all become what we were inwardly, not what we were outwardly. To this end, we are allowed to experience our outer and our inner states in turn.

When we are in our outer state, all of us are sensible—that is, we want to appear sensible—even evil people; but inwardly, evil people are insane. The succession of changes is designed to enable the evil to see their insanity and come to their senses; but if we have not come to our senses in this world we cannot do so later because we love our insanity and want to stay in it. So we make our outer nature just as insane as our inner; and in this way our inner and outer selves become one. Once this is accomplished, we are ready for hell.

On the other hand, if we are good because in the world we turned to God and came to our senses, then we have been wiser inwardly than we were outwardly. That is, outwardly we have from time to time been seduced to madness by the enticements and empty pleasures of this world. In this case, our outer nature is brought into agreement with our inner, which, as already noted, is wise. Once this has been accomplished, we are ready for heaven.

This serves to illustrate how we shed our outer nature and adopt our inner nature after death.

If [a married couple] can live together, they remain married; but if they cannot, they separate. Sometimes the husband leaves the wife, sometimes the wife leaves the husband, and sometimes they leave each other. The reason separations occur after death is that the unions formed on earth are rarely based on any inner awareness of love. Rather, they are based on a superficial aware-ness that masks what lies within. The cause and origin of this su-perficial awareness of love is found in matters involving love that is worldly and bodily in nature. Love that is worldly has to do pri-marily with wealth and possessions, while love that is bodily has to do with rank and high position. Then too, there are various se-ductive pleasures like beauty and the pretense of elegance, some-times including unchastity. Still further, marriages are contracted within the particular region, city, or town where people are born or live, where the only choices available are strictly limited to the households of acquaintances, and even more narrowly to house-holds of similar status. This is why marriages in the world are for the most part outward marriages and not inner ones at the same time; and yet it is the inner union, the union of souls, that makes a real marriage.

We cannot sense this union until we shed the outer self and adopt the inner self, which happens after death. This is why there are separations then, followed by new unions with compatible and congenial partners. There are exceptions when compatible part-ners have been provided on earth. This happens with people who from their youth have desired and longed and asked the Lord for a properly sanctioned and loving relationship with one individual, and who have rejected and turned up their noses at promiscuous desires.

[If the couple separates], a suitable wife is found for the man and a suitable husband for the woman. This is because the only married partners who can be accepted into heaven and stay there are partners who are or can be deeply united so that they are prac-tically one, because in heaven a married pair is not referred to as two angels but as one. This is the meaning of the Lord's statement that they are no longer two but are one flesh.

The reason no other married partners are accepted into heaven is that no others can live together there—in other words, can share the same house, bedroom, and bed. All the people who are in heaven are associated according to likeness and closeness of love, and this is what determines where they live. In the spiritual world, that is, there are no distances, but rather appearances of distance, and distances depend on the states of people's lives, which in turn depend on the states of their loves. This means that people cannot stay anywhere but in their own homes, homes provided and assigned according to the nature of their loves. If they stay anywhere else, their breathing becomes labored and shallow. Two people cannot live in the same house unless they are compatible; and married partners in particular must have the same priorities. If their outward priorities are not inward as well, then the house or site itself separates them, repels them, and drives them away.

This is why individuals who have been brought into heaven after due preparation are provided with marriages with partners whose souls are so drawn toward union that they want there to be one life rather than two. This is why after separating [from former partners] a man is given a suitable wife and a woman a suitable husband.

Married partners enjoy the same intercourse they did in the world, except that the pleasure and bliss are greater. However, this does not result in reproduction. Instead, there is a spiritual reproduction, a reproduction of love and wisdom. The reason married partners enjoy the same intercourse as they did in the world is that after death the male is still male and the female is still female, and a tendency to unite is an organic part of each. This human tendency is a property of the spirit and secondarily of the body, so when we become spirits after death, the same mutual tendency remains. This tendency necessarily means that there will be the same kind of intercourse. After all, we are still just as human as we were before, and nothing is missing from the male or from the female. They still have the same forms; they still have the same impulses and thoughts. What other conclusion could we draw than that they still have the same kind of intercourse? Further, since marriage love is chaste, pure, and holy, this intercourse is all-encompassing.

The reason sexual intercourse is more pleasant and blissful is that as we become spiritual this love becomes deeper and purer and therefore more aware; and every pleasure increases as awareness increases. It increases to the point that there is a perceptible bliss within the pleasure.

The reason marriages in the heavens do not result in offspring but are spiritually prolific instead—prolific of love and wisdom—is that a third element is missing for people in the spiritual world. That third element is the earthly element. This serves to contain spiritual things, and spiritual things without this container do not have the same kind of fixed identity that our offspring in the earthly world do. In and of themselves, spiritual things have to do with love and wisdom; so these are the offspring of the marriages of spiritual people.

We say that they are "offspring" because the love of marriage perfects angels. It unites one individual with another so that the angel becomes more and more human; for as already noted, two married partners in heaven are a single angel, not two angels. So their humanity is fulfilled by this marital union, which is striving to become wise, and loving what wisdom discloses.

This happens to people who get to heaven. It is different for people who end up in hell. In speaking of the man being given a suitable wife and the woman a suitable husband after death and their enjoying pleasant and blissful intercourse (but with only spiritual offspring), we must think of people who are accepted into heaven and become angels. This is because they are spiritual, and their marriages are essentially spiritual and therefore holy. In contrast, all the people who enter hell are earthly, and marriages that are solely earthly are not marriages but mere relationships, unchaste because they are based on lust.

A WEDDING IN HEAVEN

Toward evening, a messenger dressed in linen came to [a group of spirits who were being taught about life in heaven] and invited them to a wedding to be held the next day. The visitors were overjoyed at the prospect of actually seeing a wedding in heaven. . . .

When they woke up, they heard the singing of young women and girls coming from the houses on the public square. Their song gave voice to a desire for the love of marriage; and the visitors were deeply moved, struck by its beauty. They felt the blessed charm inherent in its joys, a charm that lifted the joys up and refreshed them.

When the time arrived, the angel said, "Get dressed now. Put on these heavenly clothes that the prince has sent for you." When they did, the clothes glowed with a kind of flaming light; and they asked the angel, "What's all this?" He replied, "It's because you're going to a wedding. For us, our clothes glow and become wedding garments."

Next, the angel took them to the house where the wedding was to take place and the doorkeeper opened the doors to them. Just across the threshold an angel sent by the groom cordially greeted them, brought them inside, and took them to some assigned seats. Before long, they were invited into an antechamber where they saw a table in the middle of the room holding a magnificent candelabrum with seven gold branches and candleholders. There were silver sconces on the walls that gave the atmosphere a golden glow when they were lit; and at the sides of the candelabrum they saw two tables with three rows of loaves on them. There were tables in the four corners holding crystal goblets.

While they were taking all this in, the door of a neighboring room opened, and they saw six young women come out followed by the bride and groom, hand in hand. They went to a bench near the candelabrum and sat down, the groom on the left, the bride on his right. The six young women took their places on the bride's side of the bench.

The groom was wearing a bright purple cloak and a tunic of gleaming linen, with an ephod that had a golden plate set in diamonds bearing the wedding badge of the community engraved on it, an eagle's chick. The groom's head was covered with a turban. In contrast, the bride was dressed in a scarlet cloak over an embroidered gown, in one piece from neck to feet. There was a golden belt below her chest and a golden crown set with rubies on her head.

As they were sitting there, the groom turned to the bride and placed a gold ring on her finger. Then he took a pearl necklace and bracelets and clasped the bracelets on her wrist and the necklace around her neck, saying, "Accept these as pledges." When she accepted them, he kissed her and said, "Now you are my own," and referred to her as his wife.

Once this had happened, the guests proclaimed, "Blessing!" Each did so as an individual, and then all of them together. An emissary of the prince proclaimed blessing on the prince's behalf, and at that moment the antechamber was filled with a fragrant smoke, a sign of blessing from heaven. Then servants from the two tables by the candelabrum served the loaves and the goblets from the corner tables, now filled with wine, giving each guest his or her own loaf and goblet, and everyone ate and drank.

Finally, the husband and wife rose and went to the doorway, followed by the six young women with lighted lamps in their hands. The married couple then entered the room, and the door was closed.

SEX IN HEAVEN

I ONCE SAW THREE SPIRITS, just arrived from the world, who were walking around, looking at everything, and asking questions. They were lost in wonder at the fact that they were living as persons just as before and that they were seeing the same kinds of things as before. They realized that they had left their former, earthly world and that in that world they had believed they would not live as persons until after the day of the Last Judgment, when they would be clothed in the flesh and bones that had been hidden away in their tombs. To remove all doubt that they really were persons, they kept looking closely at each other and poking themselves and each other, feeling objects, and reassuring themselves in a thousand ways that they really were persons now just as they had been in their former world. It was just that they were seeing each other in a clearer light and that everything looked more radiant and therefore more perfect.

At that point two angelic spirits happened by and engaged them in conversation. "Where are you from?"

They answered, "We have left a world and we are again living in a world, so we have gone from world to world. We're bewildered by all this." Then the three newly arrived spirits questioned the two angelic spirits about heaven. Two of the three were in their teens, and there seemed to be flickers of sexual lust in their eyes.

The angelic spirits said, "By any chance, have you seen some women?"

"We have," they said.

Since they were asking questions about heaven, the angelic spirits continued. "Everything in heaven is great and glorious. There are things that your eyes have never seen. There are young women and young men, young women so beautiful that you would call them the quintessential form of beauty, and young men of such integrity that you would call them the quintessential form of integrity. The beauty of the young women and the integrity of the young men answer to each other like mutually matching forms."

Two of the newcomers then asked whether the human forms in heaven were exactly like those in the earthly world. They were told that they were exactly alike. "Nothing is missing from the man and nothing is missing from the woman. In a word, a man is a man and a woman is a woman in that perfect form in which they were created. Step aside, if you like, and examine yourselves. See whether anything is missing that would make you less of a man than before."

The newcomers continued, "We heard in the world we have just left that in heaven people are not given in marriage because they are angels. In that case, is there any love between the sexes?"

"Your kind of love between the sexes does not exist here," the angelic spirits answered, "but there is an angelic love between the sexes that is chaste, without any of the enticement of lust."

This prompted the newcomers to say, "If there is a love between the sexes without any enticement, what kind of love is that?" and as they thought about this love they said mournfully, "What a dried-up joy heaven offers! What young man could long for that kind of heaven? Isn't a love like that barren and lifeless?"

The angelic spirits laughed and replied, "Angelic love between the sexes, the kind we have in heaven, is absolutely full of the deepest delights. The whole mind opens out with supreme pleasure, so the whole chest does as well. In the chest, it is as though the heart were at play with the lungs, a play that emerges in breath and tone and speech. This makes companionship with the other sex, companionship between young men and young women, the essence of heavenly pleasures, which are pure.

"All men who are newcomers are examined, as they come up toward heaven, to see what kind of chastity they have. They are brought into the company of young women, heavenly beauties, who sense from their tone of voice, their speech, their eyes, their body language, and the aura they emit, what kind of people they are in regard to their love for the opposite sex. If they are unchaste, the young women flee and tell their companions that they have seen satyrs or priapuses. The newcomers themselves change as well, and to angels look all hairy, with feet like calves' or leopards'. Before long, they are expelled so that their lust will not pollute the region's aura."

On hearing this, the two newcomers said again, "This means there's no love between the sexes in heaven. Chaste love between the sexes is nothing but a love emptied of its vital essence. Isn't this kind of companionship between young men and young women dried-up joy? We aren't stones and sticks, we're living feelings and impulses."

When they heard this, the angelic spirits answered indignantly, "You have no idea whatever of what chaste love between the sexes is because you aren't chaste yet. That love is the essence of delight for the mind and therefore for the heart; it does not involve the flesh beneath the heart at the same time. Angelic chastity, which is common to both sexes, prevents that love from transgressing the boundaries of the heart. Within and above those boundaries, the integrity of young men is charmed by the beauty of young women, charmed with delights of a chaste love between the sexes that are deeper and more fruitful than words can describe.

"This love between the sexes is for angels, though, because it is an extension of their love of marriage. This love cannot occur together with an unchaste love for the opposite sex. A genuine love of marriage is a chaste love that has nothing in common with unchaste love. It is a love experienced only with one member of the opposite sex apart from all others. It is a love of the spirit and then of the body, not a love of the body and then of the spirit. That is, it is not a love that attacks the spirit."

When they heard this, the two young newcomers cheered up, and said, "So there is love between the sexes here! Otherwise, what would marriage love be?" However, the angelic spirits responded, "Think seriously. Think hard, and you will discover that your kind of love between the sexes is extramarital and that a love of marriage is totally different, as different as wheat is from chaff, or better, as different as humans are from brute animals. If you ask women in heaven what extramarital love is, I assure you that they will say, 'What? What are you talking about? How can anything like that come out of your mouths? It hurts just to hear it! How can a love that was never created be begotten in a human being?' Then if you ask them what a real love of marriage is, I am sure they will tell you, 'It is not a love for the opposite sex in general but a love for one member of the opposite sex. It arises only when a young man sees the young woman the Lord has provided and the young woman sees the young man. Both feel the kindling of marital feelings in their hearts. He senses that she is his and she that he is hers. Love comes out to meet love and makes itself known, uniting their souls immediately, and later uniting their minds. From there it enters their chests, and proceeds further after the wedding. That is how it becomes a complete love, then, that grows daily to the point that they are no longer two but are to all intents and purposes one.' I know too that they will swear that this is the only kind of love for the opposite sex they know. They actually say, 'How can there be love for the opposite sex if it is not outgoing and mutual so that it longs for an eternal union, for the two to be one flesh?'"

The angelic spirits continued, "In heaven they do not even know what infidelity is. They do not know that it exists or that it is possible. Unchaste love, extramarital love, chills an angel's whole body, just as chaste love, marriage love, warms an angel's whole body. For men, their nerves sag at the approach of a prostitute and become excited at the sight of their wives."

On hearing this, the three newcomers asked, "Is there the same kind of love between married partners in the heavens as there is on earth?"

"Exactly the same," the two angelic spirits answered; and since they sensed that the newcomers wanted to know whether this involved the same kind of sexual fulfillment, they said that the sexual fulfillment of this love was exactly the same, except that it was far more blessed because angelic feeling and sensitivity is far more exquisite than human feeling and sensitivity. "What is the life of that love but a current of power? If it is lacking, won't the love fade and cool? Isn't that power the very measure, level, and foundation of that love? Isn't it the stimulus, the support, and the completion of the love? The universal law is that first things become visible, solid, and enduring because of last things. This applies to this love as well; so if there were no sexual fulfillment, there would be no trace of a love of marriage."

The newcomers then asked, "Then are children born as a result of this sexual fulfillment? And if no children are born, what use is this fulfillment?"

"No earthly offspring are born," the angelic spirits said, "but spiritual offspring are." When they were asked what spiritual offspring were, they replied, "Through their sexual fulfillment two married partners are more and more closely united in a marriage of what is good and what is true. The marriage of goodness and truth is a marriage of love and wisdom, and love and wisdom are the offspring born of this marriage. Since in this situation the husband is wisdom and the wife is its love, and since both are spiritual, the only offspring that can be conceived and born are spiritual. This is why angels are not depressed after their pleasures the way some people are on earth. Rather, they are cheerful, which happens because there is a constant flow of new vitality in place of old, both refreshing and illuminating them. Everyone who arrives in heaven returns to the springtime of her or his youth and the vitality of that age, and this lasts forever."

On hearing this, the three newcomers said, "It says in the Word that in heaven they do not have weddings because they are angels." To this the angelic spirits responded, "Look up toward heaven, and you will have your answer."

"Why should we look up toward heaven?" they asked.

"Because that is the source of all our interpretations of the Word. Inwardly, the Word is spiritual; and since angels are spiritual, they will tell us its spiritual meaning."

After a brief delay, heaven opened above their heads and two angels came into view. They said, "There are weddings in the heavens just as there are on earth, but the only weddings we have are for people who are focused on the marriage of goodness and truth. Otherwise, they are not angels at all. So the passage in question means spiritual weddings, which are marriages of goodness and truth. These happen on earth and not after death, so they do not happen in the heavens. That is the point of the story about the five foolish young women who had been invited to the wedding but couldn't gain entrance because they didn't have a marriage of goodness and truth. They had no oil, only lamps. Oil means what is good, and lamps mean what is true. Being given in marriage means gaining entrance to heaven, where that marriage is found."

The three newcomers were happy to hear this and were filled with a longing for heaven and with the hope of weddings there. "We will work on integrity and propriety of life," they said, "so that our wishes may come true."

Angelic Communication

SPIRITUAL PERCEPTION AND AURAS

AMONG THE AMAZING THINGS in the other life are perceptions, of which there are two kinds. One exists with angels: they perceive what is true and good, what comes from the Lord and what from themselves, and what the source and nature of their thoughts, words, and deeds is, when these come from themselves. The other kind is one that is common to everyone—to angels at the peak of perfection and to spirits according to their quality: as soon as another person approaches, they know what that person is like.

Let us turn to the first kind, the kind angels have—their ability to tell what is true and good, what comes from the Lord, what comes from themselves, and what the source and nature of their thoughts, words, and deeds is, when these come from themselves.

I was allowed to talk with the descendants of the earliest church about their ability to perceive. They said they did not and could not think anything on their own or will anything on their own. With each and every thought or impulse, they said, they can tell what comes from the Lord and what comes from somewhere else. They perceive not only how much is from the Lord and how much is seemingly from themselves but also (when it does seem to originate in themselves) where it comes from. That is, they perceive which angels it comes from, what those angels are like, what all their different thoughts are, and so what the various influences are, along with countless other factors.

Perceptions of this kind come in many varieties. Heavenly angels, who love the Lord, perceive goodness, and this enables them to perceive everything that is a matter of truth. Since they perceive truth from the standpoint of what is good, they do not allow any discussion of truth (let alone argument about it) but say yes or no. Spiritual angels, on the other hand, who also have perception (though not the kind heavenly angels have), do talk about truth and goodness. They still perceive things, but they perceive them in many different ways, because this kind of perception has countless variations. The variations have to do with perceiving whether the Lord wills a thing or accepts it or tolerates it—which are quite different from each other.

There are spirits who want to argue everything. They do not perceive what is good or true, and in fact the more they argue, the less they perceive it. They identify wisdom with sophistry, which they count on to make them seem wise. I told them that the role of angelic wisdom is to perceive whether a thing is good or true without sophistic reasoning, but they cannot grasp the possibility that this kind of perception exists. They are the same people that used the academic and philosophical disciplines during bodily life to cast confusion over truth and goodness and as a result seemed to themselves to be more knowledgeable than others. (They had not started with any valid assumptions taken from the Word.) Consequently, they do not have much common sense.

As long as spirits imagine that they lead themselves, and that they think for themselves and gain knowledge, intelligence, and wisdom for themselves, they cannot have perception. Instead they consider perception to be stuff and nonsense.

Several times I have talked about perception with people in the next life who while they were living in the world had imagined they could investigate and understand any subject. "Angels," I said, "perceive that they think and speak and that they will and act from the Lord."

The people I was talking to, though, could not comprehend what perception was. They thought that if everything were the result of outside influence like this, it would rob them completely of life, because it would mean never thinking for themselves, never thinking independently—which for them was life. It would mean that someone else was thinking for them and not they themselves. So they would be mere instruments, devoid of life.

"The difference in quality of life between having perception and not having it," I pointed out, "is like night and day. You first start to live your own life when you receive this perception, because you then live from the Lord. You then enjoy a sense of individuality as well, which comes to you replete with every happiness and joy."

From plentiful experience, I also illustrated for them how perception works, and they then acknowledged that it was possible. After a while, though, they again forgot, doubted, and denied. This showed me how hard it is for people to grasp what perception is.

The second kind of perception, as already mentioned, is one that is common to everyone—to angels at the peak of perfection and to spirits according to their quality. As soon as another person approaches, they know what that person is like, even if the person says nothing. It reveals itself instantaneously, by a sort of inspiration that is most amazing. Good spirits are recognized not only for the type of goodness they have but also for the type of belief. When they talk, it comes through in every word. Evil spirits are recognized for their wickedness and unbelief, and when they talk, it comes through in every word. The clues are so plain as to be unmistakable.

Something similar can be seen with people on earth. They too can sometimes tell what others are thinking from the gestures, facial expression, and speech of those others, even when their words contradict it. This skill in humans is an earthly one whose origin can be traced to a character trait in spirits that grants them the same ability, and so to an individual's own spirit and its communication with the world of spirits. This shared perception originates in the Lord's wish that all blessings spread contagiously and that everyone enjoy mutual love and grow happy as a result. That is why this type of perception also prevails everywhere among spirits.

Souls that had arrived in the other life once expressed their surprise to find that another person's thoughts are communicated in this way. They were also amazed that they could instantly tell not only what kind of character that other person had but also what the person's beliefs were.

I told them that spirits receive abilities far superior once they separate from their bodies. During physical life, objects of the senses have an impact on us, as do fantasies built out of the impressions those objects leave on our memory, not to mention worries about the future; various cravings aroused by external stimuli;

concern over food, clothes, housing, and children; and so on. People in the other life never think about any of these things. When such thoughts are set aside as obstacles and barriers, together with bodily desires connected to the coarser sensations, people cannot help being in a more ideal condition. Their former abilities remain but become much more perfect, lucid, and free. This is especially true with people who have lived lives of charity and faith in the Lord, and of innocence. Their capacities are heightened tremendously over the ones they had in the body, until finally their gifts match those of angels in the third heaven.

It is not only the feelings and thoughts of others that are shared but their knowledge as well. So widely is knowledge shared that each spirit thinks he or she already knows what the next spirit knows, even if the first spirit had previously known nothing about the subject. Everything that others know about accordingly becomes common property. Some spirits retain the knowledge, some do not.

Spirits share these things with each other in conversation and through mental images accompanied by visual representations. The images that compose their thoughts also take visible form, you see, which allows everything to be presented in full detail. Spirits can depict more through a single mental image than they can express in a thousand words. Angels even perceive what lies behind the image, what feeling is connected with it, where that feeling comes from, what the purpose of it is, and many other inner aspects.

It is also common in the other world for one person to communicate pleasure and happiness in a remarkable way by actually passing them on to a number of others, who are as much affected by them as the original person. The communication takes place without any lessening of the feelings in the person who shares them to begin with..

I too was given the opportunity to share my pleasure with others by transferring it to them.

You can imagine, then, what kind of happiness exists in people who love their neighbor more than themselves and want nothing more than to spread their happiness to others. Their attitude traces its origin to the Lord, who communicates happiness to angels in the same way.

When people share happiness, they are constantly passing it along in the way just described, but they do so without reflecting on their active role in the process and without making a conscious, deliberate decision to engage in it.

Another astonishing way happiness spreads is through extraction—a process whose nature cannot be grasped by people on earth. Harsh, disturbing elements are removed in an instant, and in the process, something pleasing and happy is presented, with nothing to block it. Once any hindrances are removed, angels stream in and communicate their joy.

Since perception allows one person to see immediately what kind of love and belief another has, people come together in communities insofar as they harmonize, and separate insofar as they conflict. The process is so precise that not the smallest variation fails either to divide or to unite. As a result, communities in the heavens have distinctive characters—as distinct as anyone could possibly imagine. The differences depend on variations in love for the Lord and faith in him, which are countless. From this comes the form of heaven, which is such that it resembles a single human. That form is constantly being perfected.

A wealth of experience has taught me how this kind of perception works, but recounting all of it would take too long. . . .

All spirits have contact with the inner heaven and the inmost (although they are unaware of it); otherwise they could not live. Their inner nature is recognized by angels, who are awake to deeper dimensions, and the Lord also governs them through angels. So their inner characteristics become common knowledge in heaven, as their outer ones do in the world of spirits.

These inner communications adapt each of them for some useful role, and they are drawn to that role without realizing it.

The situation with people on earth is the same. We too communicate through angels with heaven—in complete ignorance of the fact that we do—because otherwise we could not live. (The influence heaven has on our thinking is merely the outermost effect of that interaction.) Such contact is the source of all our life, and it regulates everything we try to do in life. . . .

In the other life, as mentioned, one individual recognizes another's character as soon as that other approaches, even if she or he says nothing. This experience reveals the fact that our inward reaches are somehow active (although we are unaware of it) and that their activity enables others to perceive what kind of spirit we are. I was able to see the truth of this by observing that the aura of this activity not only radiates far and wide but sometimes (when the Lord allows) makes itself perceptible in various ways.

In addition, I learned how we acquire these auras, which become so tangible in the other world. To put it in comprehensible terms, take the example of people who have formed an opinion of themselves as superior to others. They eventually develop the habit and the instinct, so to speak, of focusing on themselves whenever they see other people or talk to them, wherever they go. They do so consciously at first and then unconsciously, so that they themselves become blind to it. Still, the habit governs every one of their gestures and words, just as it governs every one of their feelings and thoughts. This is something we are capable of noticing in others. Such a trait is what creates an aura in the next life, and others perceive the aura, but no more often than the Lord allows.

The same is true with other attitudes as well. As a result, there are as many auras as there are moods and combinations of mood, which are countless. Our aura is like an image of ourselves projected outside us. In fact it is an image of everything inside us. What presents itself to view or to perception in the world of spirits, however, is only a general approximation. In heaven, on the other hand, our character is recognized in a more specific way. No one but the Lord, though, knows what we are like down to the smallest details.

Let me relate several experiences illustrating the nature of auras.

A certain spirit I had known and talked to when he lived in his body later appeared many times in the company of evil spirits. Because he had a high opinion of himself, he had developed an air of superiority to others. And because he was like this, the other spirits suddenly fled, so that none but he could be seen. He then filled up his whole environment in all directions, and the atmosphere was one of concentration on himself. Soon afterward, abandoned by fellow members of his own community as well, he sank into another state. (Those in the other life who are deserted by the community in which they live seem to become half dead at first.

At that point, the only thing that keeps them alive is the influence of heaven on their inward capacities.) Then he began to complain and to suffer.

Other spirits later told me that they could not stand to have him near, because he considered himself more important than anyone else. Eventually, having formed ties with a new community, he rose high up and consequently seemed to himself to be governing the universe all alone. (Those are the lengths to which self-love inflates our pride when left to itself.) Afterward he was thrown down among hellish spirits. Such is the lot that awaits those who consider themselves greater than others. More than any other love, self-love is opposed to mutual love, which is the life of heaven.

There was one person who in bodily life had viewed himself as greater and wiser than others, although in other respects he had been honorable enough, not holding other people in contempt on that account. Because he had been born to high position, however, he had developed an air of prestige and power.

As such he came to me and for a long time said nothing. I noticed, though, that he was surrounded by a kind of fog, which drifted out from him and started to envelop other spirits and then to distress them. Speaking to me from inside it, they said that they could not possibly stay there, that they were being robbed of all freedom, so that they did not dare to say anything. He too began to talk and addressed them, calling them his children and at various times instructing them, but always with the authority that he had acquired.

This experience showed me what an aura of personal power is like in the other world.

I had many opportunities to observe that people who had been endowed with the highest positions in the world inevitably took on an air of authority as a result. Consequently they were unable to hide it or cast it off in the other life. In the ones who have received the gift of faith and of love for others, the air of authority combines in a miraculous way with one of benevolence, so that it disturbs no one. In fact well-mannered spirits also offer them a kind of corresponding deference. The atmosphere they give off is not a dictatorial one; it is just an aura natural to them, because they were born that way. Since they are good, and since they work at shedding that aura, after a certain amount of time they succeed.

For several days I had with me the kind of spirits who had not concentrated at all on the good of society when they lived in the world but on themselves. They had been useless, so far as political office goes, and their only goal had been to live sumptuously, wear glamorous clothes, and grow rich. They were used to putting up pretenses; to finding means of worming their way in everywhere by various kinds of flattery; and to vying for office with the sole purpose of making themselves visible and taking charge of their overlord's resources. Anyone engaged in any serious kind of work they regarded with contempt. They had been courtiers, I perceived.

The effect they had was to sap me of all my energy and to make it burdensome for me to act on or think about anything worthwhile, anything true or good—so terribly burdensome that in the end I hardly knew what to do.

When spirits like this come among other spirits, they infect them with a similar sluggishness. In the other life, they are useless members of society and are rejected wherever they go.

Every spirit and to a greater extent every community of spirits has its own aura, formed from and given off by the assumptions and self-deceptions that it has adopted. (Demons have an aura formed by their longings.)

By its inherent nature, when one person's aura of assumptions and self-deceptions influences another person, it makes truth appear to be false. It also stirs up all kinds of supportive ideas, so that it convinces the person to accept falsity as true and evil as good. (This fact made it clear to me how easily we can become entrenched in falsity and evil, unless we believe the truth that comes from the Lord.) Such auras are denser or thinner, depending on the nature of the falsities.

These auras are completely out of harmony with the auras of spirits who subscribe to the truth. If the two kinds of aura come near each other, war breaks out. If the atmosphere of falsity is permitted to win, the good spirits come into times of trial and anguish. . . .

Much experience has taught me to recognize—and to recognize as clearly as I recognize anything—that spirits who are caught up in falsity influence our thinking and thoroughly convince us that falsity is true. We cannot see it any other way, and this results from their aura.

Demons too, who are immersed in evil, influence our will in this way and cause evil to seem utterly good. We cannot feel it any other way, and this again results from their aura.

I have had a thousand opportunities to perceive clearly the influence of each group, to tell who it came from, how angels working for the Lord removed the effects, and many other details besides, which cannot well be listed individually.

From this I could see two things with such certainty that nothing has ever seemed more certain to me. One is where the falsity and evil in us come from. The other is the fact that false assumptions and the desire for evil give rise to these auras that stay with us after physical life has ended and that display themselves so openly. . . .

Auras also present themselves to the senses through odors, which spirits are much more keenly sensitive to than people on earth are. In fact auras correspond to smells, amazingly enough.

Some people have indulged in humbug, which has given them their character. When their aura is turned into a smell, it stinks like vomit.

Some have learned to speak elegantly in order to impress others with everything they say. When their aura takes on an odor, it resembles the smell of burnt bread.

Some have indulged in mere physical pleasure, without developing any neighborly love or any faith. Their aura smells like excrement.

The same is true of those who have carried out a life filled with adultery, although their stench is even worse.

Some have lived lives of intense hatred and vengefulness and of cruelty. When their aura is turned into a smell, it reeks like a corpse.

The smell of rats wafts from those who have been disgustingly greedy.

The smell of household vermin drifts from those who have persecuted the innocent.

These smells cannot be picked up by any earthly person except one whose inner senses have been opened to allow companionship with spirits.

I perceived the aura of stench from a certain woman who later joined a group of sirens, and the stench emanated from her wherever she went for a period of several days. The spirits said that the reek was almost lethal, but still the woman herself did not smell it at all.

Sirens have essentially the same foul smell, since their inner depths are revolting, although their outer looks are mostly attractive and fetching. . . .

When heavenly angels are present with the body of a dead person who is to be revived, the smell of the body turns into a sweet fragrance, and once evil spirits smell it, they cannot come close.

When an aura of charity or faith is perceived as a smell, it yields intense pleasure. The smell is sweet, like the smell of flowers, of lilies, of different types of perfume, with unlimited variety.

An angel's aura can also be displayed visibly, as an atmosphere or nimbus, and these are so beautiful, so sweet, and so full of variety that they could never be described.

However, although I have been talking about the way a spirit's inner dimensions can be perceived through auras radiating from and generated by the spirit, and through smells too, it needs to be known that these indicators do not display themselves all the time. In addition, the Lord modifies them in various ways, to keep a spirit's character from lying open to others' view all the time.

THE LANGUAGE OF ANGELS

ANGELS TALK WITH EACH OTHER just the way we do in this world. They talk about various things—domestic matters, community concerns, issues of moral life, and issues of spiritual life. There is no difference except that they talk with each other more intelligently than we do because they talk from a deeper level of thought.

I have often been allowed to be in their company and talk with them like one friend with another, or sometimes like one stranger with another; and since at such times I was in a state like theirs, it seemed exactly as though I were talking with people on earth.

Angelic language, like human language, is differentiated into words. It is similarly uttered audibly and heard audibly. Angels have mouths and tongues and ears just as we do; and they also have an atmosphere in which the sound of their language is articulated. However, it is a spiritual atmosphere that is adapted to angels, who are spiritual. Angels breathe in their atmosphere and use their breath to utter words just the way we do in ours.

All people in heaven have the same language. They all understand each other, no matter what community they come from, whether nearby or remote. This language is not learned but is innate; it flows from their very affection and thought. The sound of the language corresponds to their affection and the articulations of the sound—the words, that is—correspond to the mental constructs that arise from their affections. Since their language corresponds to these [inner events], it too is spiritual, for it is audible affection and vocal thinking.

Anyone who reflects may realize that all thought comes from affection, which is a function of love, and that mental constructs are various forms into which the general affection is apportioned; for no thoughts or concepts whatever occur apart from affection. This is the source of their soul and life. This is why angels know simply from speech what kind of person someone is—they know the quality of the affection from the sound and the quality of the mind from the articulations of the sound, or words. Wiser angels know from a single series of statements what someone's ruling affection is, since this is what they are primarily attentive to.

It is recognized that all people have various affections or moods—one in times of happiness, another in times of sorrow, another in times of tenderness and compassion, another in times of honesty and truth, another in times of love and thoughtfulness, another in times of zeal or anger, another in times of pretense and guile, another in times of ambition for respect and adulation, and so on; but there is a dominant affection or love within all of these, so since the wiser angels perceive this, they know from conversation the whole state of another person.

I have been granted knowledge of this through an abundance of experience. I have heard angels discover a person's life simply by listening. They have told me that they know everything about another person's life from a few individual ideas because these enable them to know the person's ruling love, which contains everything in a pattern. This is all that our "book of life" is.

Angelic language has nothing in common with human language except with a few of our words whose sound reflects some feeling, and in this case not with the words themselves but with their sound, which will be further dealt with later.

The fact that angelic language has nothing in common with human language is evidenced by angels' inability to pronounce a single word of a human language. It has been tried, and they could not. The only things they can utter are the ones that are in complete accord with their own affection. Anything that does not agree offends their very life, since their life is a matter of affection and their language flows from it.

I have been told that the first language of people on our earth shared this nature because it was given them from heaven, and that Hebrew resembles it in some respects.

Since angels' language corresponds to the affections of their love, and since heaven's love is love for the Lord and love for our neighbor, we can see how elegant and delightful their conversation is. It affects not only the ears but also the deeper levels of the minds of those who hear it. There was one particular hard-hearted spirit with whom an angel talked, and eventually he was so moved by what the angel was saying that he burst into tears, saying that he couldn't help it, love was talking, and he had never cried before.

The language of angels is also full of wisdom, since it flows from the deeper levels of their thought and their deeper thought is wisdom the way their deeper affection is love. Their love and wisdom unite in speech. As a result, it is so full of wisdom that they can in a single word express what we cannot say in a thousand words; and the concepts of their thinking can encompass things the like of which we cannot grasp, let alone articulate. This is why the things that have been heard and seen in heaven are called inexpressible, such as ear has never heard, nor eye seen.

I have been granted knowledge of this through experience as well. At times I have been conveyed into the state in which angels are and have talked with them in that state. At such times I understood everything, but when I returned to my original state and therefore into the normal thought processes of physical consciousness and wanted to recall what I had heard, I could not. There were a thousand things that would not fit into natural ideas and were therefore inexpressible except by subtle shifts of heavenly light, and not at all, then, in human words.

The individual ideas of angels that give rise to their words are also variations in heaven's light; and the affections that give rise to the sounds of the words are variations of heaven's warmth. This is because heaven's light is divine truth or wisdom and heaven's warmth is divine good or love, and angels receive their affection from divine love and their thought from divine wisdom.

Because angels' language flows directly from their affection (since their individual ideas are various forms into which their affections are apportioned), angels can express in a minute more than we can say in half an hour, and can present in a few words things that would make many pages of writing. This too has been witnessed to me by a great deal of experience.

Angels' individual ideas and the words of their language form a single whole the way an efficient cause does with an effect; for what is presented in the words as an effect is what is resident in the ideas as a cause. This is why a single word contains so much within itself.

When the details of angels' thought and the consequent details of their language are presented in visual form, they look like a subtle wave or flowing atmosphere in which there are countless elements in their own pattern, elements of their wisdom that enter into thought at a higher level and stir the affections. The individual ideas of anyone—whether an angel or one of us—can be presented visually in heaven's light when it so pleases the Lord.

Angels who live in the Lord's heavenly kingdom talk much the same way as angels who are citizens of the Lord's spiritual kingdom. However, heavenly angels talk from a deeper level of thought than spiritual angels do. Further, since heavenly angels are attuned to the good of love for the Lord, they talk from wisdom, while spiritual angels—being attuned to the good of thoughtfulness toward their neighbor (which in its essence is truth)—talk from intelligence. For wisdom comes from what is good and intelligence from what is true.

The speech of heavenly angels is like a gentle stream, soft and virtually unbroken, while the speech of spiritual angels is a little more resonant and crisp. Then too, the vowels *U* and *O* tend to predominate in the speech of heavenly angels, while in the speech of spiritual angels it is the vowels *E* and *I*. The vowels stand for the sound and in the sound there is the affection; for as already noted, the sound of angels' speech is responsive to their affection, and the articulations of the sound, or the words, correspond to the individual ideas that stem from their affection. For this reason, the vowels do not belong to the language but to a raising of its words, by means of sounds, toward various affections according to the state of each individual. So in Hebrew the vowels are not written and are also pronounced variously. This enables angels to recognize what someone's quality is in respect to affection and love.

Further still, the language of heavenly angels lacks any hard consonants and rarely puts two consonants together without inserting a word that begins with a vowel. This is why the little word *and* is inserted so often in the Word, as can be determined by people who read the Word in Hebrew, in which language that word is soft and in either pronunciation is a vowel sound. We can also learn some of this from the vocabulary of the Hebrew Bible, since the words belong to either a heavenly or a spiritual category. That is, they involve either what is good or what is true, with the expressions involving what is good making ample use of the vowels *U* and *O* and to some extent *A,* and the expressions involving what is true making use of *E* and *I.*

Since affections are expressed primarily through sounds, words that use *U* and *O* are well loved in human language to express great matters like heaven and God. Musical sounds tend in this direction as they rise, when they are dealing with such matters, but not when they are dealing with lesser things. This is why the art of music is so adept at expressing various kinds of affection.

There is a certain concord in angelic speech that is indescribable. This concord stems from the fact that the thoughts and affections that give rise to speech flow forth and spread out in keeping with heaven's form, heaven's form being what determines how everyone there associates and communicates.

The same kind of speech we find in the spiritual world is innate in all of us, but in the deeper part of our intellect. However, since for us it does not come down into words that parallel our affections the way it does for angels, we are unaware that we possess it. Yet this is why we have access to the same language as spirits and angels when we arrive in the other life and know how to talk with them without being taught. But more on this below.

There is, as already noted, a single language for everyone in heaven; but it does vary, in that the language of wiser people is more profound and more full of shades of affections and specific concepts. The language of less wise individuals is less profound and not so full, and the language of simple people is still less profound, actually consisting of words that yield meaning only the way they do when we on earth talk with each other.

There is also a language of facial expressions that switch over to a sound modified by ideas, and a language in which images of heaven are combined with concepts and the concepts are presented visually. There is also a language of bodily movements responsive to affections and portraying the same things that their verbal expressions do. There is a language of shared affections and of shared thoughts; there is a thunderous language; and there are other languages as well.

The language of evil and hellish spirits is much the same, because it too stems from their affections, but it comes from evil affections and their foul concepts, which are utterly repugnant to angels. This means that the languages of hell are opposite to the languages of heaven. Evil people cannot stand angelic speech, and angels cannot stand hellish speech. To angels, hellish speech is like a rank odor that assaults the nostrils.

The language of hypocrites—people who can imitate angels of light—is like that of angels as far as its words are concerned, but exactly opposite in respect to its affections and their individual thoughts. So when the inner quality of their speech is perceived, as it is by wise angels, it sounds like a grinding of teeth and strikes horror into them.

HOW ANGELS TALK WITH US

ANGELS WHO TALK WITH US do not talk in their own language but in ours, or in other languages in which we may be fluent—not in languages of which we have no knowledge. The reason for this is that when angels talk with us they turn toward us and unite with us; and one consequence of this union is that the two parties have much the same thought processes. Since our thinking is closely allied with our memory, and our language flows from it, the two parties share the same language. Further, when angels or spirits come to us and unite with us by turning toward us, they enter into our whole memory so completely that it seems exactly as though they themselves know everything we know, including our languages.

I have talked with angels about this and said that they might suppose they were talking with me in my own mother tongue simply because it seemed that way, when in fact it was not they talking but I. This follows from the fact that angels cannot utter a single word of our human language, as noted above. Then too, human language is natural and they are spiritual, and spiritual beings cannot produce anything natural. They have answered that they knew that when they were talking with us their union with us was with our spiritual thinking, but since this spiritual thinking flowed into our natural thought, and this natural thinking is so closely allied with our memory, it seemed to them as though our language were their own, along with all our acquired knowledge. This is because it has pleased the Lord that there should be this kind of union and inner presence of heaven with us. However, they said, the state of humanity is now such that this kind of union is no longer with angels but with spirits who are not in heaven.

I have talked with spirits about this matter, too; but they wanted to believe not that we were talking but that they were talking within us, so that we did not really know what we know, but they did, which meant that everything we knew came from them. I wanted to convince them by many arguments that this was not the case but failed.

The reason angels and spirits are so intimately united to us that it seems to them as though our characteristics were their own is that there is such an intimate union within us of the spiritual and the natural worlds that they are virtually one. However, because we have separated ourselves from heaven, the Lord has provided that there should be angels and spirits with each of us and that we should be governed by the Lord through them. This is the reason there is such an intimate union.

It would have been different if we had not separated ourselves, because then we could have been governed by the Lord through a general inflow from heaven without having spirits and angels assigned to us.

When angels and spirits talk with us, it sounds just as audible as when we talk with each other, but it is not audible to people who are nearby, only to ourselves. This is because the speech of an angel or spirit flows first into our thought and then by an inner route into our organ of hearing so that it activates it from within. Our speech with each other flows first into the air and comes to our organ of hearing and activates it by an outward route. We can see from this that the speech of an angel or spirit with us is heard within us, and that since it activates our hearing mechanism just as much [as our speech with each other does], it is just as audible.

The fact that the speech of an angel or spirit flows down into the ear from within has been made clear to me from the way it flowed into my tongue as well and made it tremble slightly, though not with the actual motion involved when we are articulating the sounds of speech in the formation of words. . . .

Conversation with angels is not granted, though, except to people who are focused on truths that flow from good intent, especially people who acknowledge the Lord and the divine nature within his human nature, because this is the truth in which heaven exists. For [as discussed in my work *Heaven and Hell*] the Lord is heaven's God; the Lord's divine nature makes heaven; the Lord's divine nature in heaven is love for him and thoughtfulness from him toward one's neighbor; and the whole heaven, grasped as a single entity, reflects a single individual, as does each community of heaven; and each individual angel has a perfect human form because of the Lord's divine human nature. We can see from this that conversation with angels is not granted except to people whose deeper levels have been opened by divine truths all the way to the Lord, since it is into these that the Lord flows within us, and when the Lord flows in, so does heaven.

The reason divine truths open our deeper levels is that we have been so created that our inner person is an image of heaven and our outer an image of the world; and our inner person is opened only by the divine truth that emanates from the Lord, because this is the light and the life of heaven.

The inflow of the Lord himself into us is into the forehead and from there into the whole face. The inflow of the spiritual angels who are with us is into our head overall, from the forehead and temples to the whole region that covers the cerebrum, because this area corresponds to our intelligence. In contrast, the inflow of heavenly angels is into the part of the head that covers the cerebellum and is called the occiput, from one ear to the other and down to the neck, since this area corresponds to our wisdom.

All the speech of angels comes into our thoughts by these two paths. This has enabled me to notice just which angels were talking with me.

People who talk with heaven's angels also see the things that are in heaven because they are seeing in that light of heaven that surrounds their inner levels. Not only that, through them angels see things that are on our earth. For people who talk with angels, heaven is actually united to our world and our world to heaven; for as already noted, when angels turn toward us they unite themselves with us so completely that it seems to them exactly as though whatever is ours is actually theirs. This applies not only to elements of our language but to what is involved in our sight and hearing. In addition, it seems to us exactly as though the things that are flowing in through the angels are really ours.

The earliest humans on our planet enjoyed this kind of union with heaven's angels, which is why their times are called the Golden Age. Because they acknowledged the Divine in human form and therefore were acknowledging the Lord, they talked with heaven's angels as they did with members of their own family, and heaven's angels talked with them in the same way; and in them heaven and this world were a single whole.

But after those times, people moved step by step away from heaven by loving themselves more than the Lord and the world more than heaven. So they began to feel the pleasures of self-love and love of the world separately from the pleasures of heaven, ultimately to the point where they did not know there was any other kind of pleasure. Then their deeper levels were closed, the levels that open into heaven, while their outer levels were open to the world. Once this has happened, we are in the light in respect to everything in this world and in darkness in respect to everything in heaven.

Since those times people have seldom talked with heaven's angels, though some have talked with spirits who are not in heaven. Our inner and outer levels can by their nature be turned toward the Lord as their common center, or toward ourselves and therefore away from the Lord. The ones that are turned toward the Lord are also turned toward heaven, while the ones that are turned toward ourselves are also turned toward this world; and the ones that are turned in this latter direction are hard to raise up. Still, they are raised up by the Lord to the extent that they can be, through a turning of our love; and this is accomplished by means of truths from the Word.

I have been told how the Lord spoke to the prophets through whom the Word was written. He did not talk with them the way he did with the early people, by an inflow into their deeper natures, but through spirits sent to them whom the Lord filled with his appearance. In this way, he inspired them with the words that they in turn told to the prophets, so that it was not a case of inflow but of direct command. Since at that time the words were coming directly from the Lord, the very details are filled with the Divine and contain within themselves an inner meaning of such nature that heaven's angels take them in a heavenly and spiritual meaning while we are taking them in a natural meaning. In this way, the Lord unites heaven and earth through the Word.

I have also been shown how the Lord fills spirits with his divine nature by means of his appearance. Spirits filled with the Divine by the Lord have no sense whatever that they are not actually the Lord or that it is not the Lord who is speaking, which lasts as long as they are talking. Afterward they realize and admit that they are spirits and that they were not talking on their own, but from the Lord.

Because this was the state of the spirits who talked with the prophets, they themselves said that Jehovah was talking. The spirits actually called themselves "Jehovah," as can be seen not only in the prophetic books but also in the historical books of the Word.

To illustrate what the union of angels and spirits with us is like, I may cite a few memorable instances that will serve to illuminate the subject and enable some conclusions to be drawn. When angels and spirits turn toward us, it seems to them exactly as though our language were their own and that they have no other. This is because they are involved in our language at such times, and do not even remember their own. The moment they turn away from us, though, they are back in their own angelic and spiritual language and have no knowledge whatever of ours. The same thing has happened with me when I have been in the company of angels and in a state like theirs. Then I have talked with them in their language and knew nothing of my own. I could not even remember it. However, the moment I was no longer in their company I was back in my own language.

It is also worth noting that when angels and spirits turn toward us, they can talk with us even from a great distance. They have talked with me from far off just as audibly as though they were nearby. Still, when they turn away from us and talk with each other, nothing of what they say is audible to us even though this is happening right next to our ears. This has enabled me to see that in the spiritual world, all union depends on the way people are facing.

Again, it is worth noting that many of them can talk with one of us at the same time, and that person with them. They send some particular spirit from themselves to the individual with whom they want to talk, and this envoy spirit turns toward the person while the others turn toward their [envoy] spirit and so concentrate their thoughts, which the spirit then presents. It seems to such envoys entirely as though they were talking on their own, and to the others as though they themselves were. So a union of several with one is achieved by the way they face.

No angel or spirit is allowed to talk with one of us from the angel's or spirit's own memory, only from that of the individual in question. Angels and spirits actually have memory just as we do. If a spirit were to talk with us from his or her own memory, then it would seem to us entirely as though the thoughts were our own, when they would really belong to the spirit. It is like remembering something that we have never seen or heard. I have been granted knowledge of the truth of this by experience.

This is why some of the ancients were of the opinion that after some thousands of years they would return to their former life and all its deeds, and that they had in fact returned. They gathered this from the fact that sometimes a kind of memory would come up of things that they had never seen or heard. This happened because spirits had flowed from their own memory into the images of these people's thoughts.

There are also spirits called natural and physical spirits who do not unite with our thoughts when they come to us the way other spirits do but rather enter our bodies and take over all its senses, talking through our mouths and acting through our limbs. It seems to them entirely as though everything of ours were theirs. These are the spirits that possess people; but they have been cast into hell by the Lord and moved decisively away; so possession like this no longer occurs nowadays.

WE ARE ALWAYS IN CONTACT WITH
HEAVEN AND HELL

IT IS ACKNOWLEDGED IN THE CHURCH that everything good comes from God and nothing of it from us, and therefore that we should never take personal credit for anything good. It is also recognized that evil comes from the devil. This is why people who talk from the doctrine of the church describe people who are acting well and who are talking devoutly and preaching as being led by God, and say the opposite about people who are acting maliciously and speaking blasphemously. None of this could happen unless we had a union with heaven and a union with hell, and unless those unions were with our volition and our understanding, since it is from these that the body acts and the mouth speaks. We need now to describe what this union is like.

There are good spirits and evil spirits with every individual. We have our union with heaven through the good spirits and our union with hell through the evil ones. These spirits are in the world of spirits, which is intermediate between heaven and hell.

When these spirits come to us, they come into our whole memory and from there into all our thinking—evil spirits into the matters of memory and thought that are evil, and good spirits into the matters of memory and thought that are good. These spirits are totally unaware that they are with us. Rather, as long as they are, they believe that all these matters of our memory and thought are actually theirs. They do not see us, either, because their sight does not extend to things in our subsolar world.

The Lord takes the greatest care to prevent spirits from knowing whom they are with. If they did know, they would talk with them, and then the evil spirits would destroy them; for evil spirits, being united to hell, want nothing more than to destroy us not only as to spirit (that is, as to our love and faith) but as to our bodies as well. It is different when they do not talk with us. Then they do not know that we are the source of what they are thinking—and what they are saying to each other, since they talk to each other just the way we do—but believe that these matters are their own. They value and love whatever is their own, so these spirits are constrained to love and value us, even though they do not know it.

This kind of union has become so familiar to me through years of constant experience as to be commonplace.

The reason spirits who are in touch with hell are attached to us as well is that we are born into all kinds of evil, so that our first life is made up of nothing else. Unless spirits of the same kind were associated with us, then, we could not live or be led out of our evils and reformed. So we are kept in our own life by evil spirits and restrained from it by good spirits. Through the two kinds, we are kept in a balance; and since we are in a balance we enjoy an appropriate measure of freedom and can be led out of our evils and turned toward good. This good can be sown in us as well, which could never happen except in our freedom; and the freedom could not be granted us unless spirits from hell were acting on the one side and spirits from heaven on the other, with us in the middle.

I have been shown that to the extent that we exist from our hereditary nature and from ourselves, we could have no life at all if we were not allowed to engage in evil. We would also have no life if we were not in some freedom, and we cannot be compelled to good: anything compelled does not become part of us. I have also been shown that anything good that we accept in freedom is sown in our intentions and becomes virtually our own. This is why we have a communication with hell and a communication with heaven. . . .

The kind of spirit that is associated with us is determined by the kind of person we are in respect to affection and love, though good spirits are assigned to us by the Lord while we ourselves summon the evil ones. The spirits with us change, however, as our own affections change. This means we have one kind with us in infancy, another kind during our childhood, another kind as we are growing up and in early adulthood, and still another kind in old age. During our earliest years, spirits who are in innocence are with us, that is, spirits who are in touch with the heaven of innocence, the inmost or third heaven. In later childhood we are in the company of spirits who are engaged in an affection for knowledge and who are in touch with the ultimate or first heaven. As we are growing up, during our early adulthood, spirits who are responsive to affections for what is true and good and therefore with intelligence are with us. They are spirits who are in touch with the second or intermediate heaven. In old age, though, spirits who are in wisdom and innocence are with us, spirits therefore who are in touch with the inmost or third heaven.

Still, this association is arranged by the Lord for people who can be reformed and regenerated. It is different for people who cannot be reformed or regenerated. Good spirits are assigned to them as well in order to restrain them from evil as much as possible, but their direct connection is with the evil spirits who are in touch with hell. This means that the spirits are of the same nature as the people they are associated with. Whether they love themselves or money or revenge or adultery, the same kind of spirits are with them and are, so to speak, taking up residence in their evil affections. To the extent that we cannot be restrained from evil by good spirits, they inflame us, and to the extent that an evil affection is in control, they cling to us and will not back off.

In this way, evil people are united to hell and good people to heaven.

The reason we are controlled by the Lord through spirits is that we are not in the pattern of heaven. We are in fact born into evils that are from hell and are therefore exactly opposite to the divine pattern. This means that we need to be brought back into the pattern, and we cannot be brought back except through the agency of spirits. It would be different if we were born into the good that accords with heaven's pattern. Then we would not be controlled by the Lord through the agency of spirits but through the pattern itself and therefore through a general inflow.

This [general] inflow determines the way things move from thought and intent into act and therefore determines our speech and actions, since these both do flow according to a natural pattern. So the spirits who are with us have nothing to do with these processes.

Animals are also controlled through a general inflow from the spiritual world because they are in the pattern proper to their life, a pattern that they can neither distort nor destroy, because they do not have a rational faculty.

To continue with the general topic of the union of heaven with the human race, we need to be aware that the Lord flows into each one of us according to heaven's design, into our inmost natures as well as into our outmost, and disposes us to accept heaven. He controls our outmost natures from the inmost and the inmost from the outmost at the same time, and in this way keeps everything about us in coherent connection. This inflow from the Lord is called a direct inflow, while a second inflow that happens through the agency of spirits is called an indirect inflow. The latter is sustained by the former. The direct inflow, an action of the Lord himself, is from his divine human. It comes into our intentions, and through our intentions into our understanding. This means it comes into what is good in us and through that good into what is true in us, or (which amounts to the same thing) into our love and through our love into our faith. It does not happen the other way around, much less into faith apart from love or into truth apart from good or into understanding apart from volition.

This divine inflow is unceasing and is accepted in what is good in good people, but not in evil ones. In them it is either rejected or stifled or distorted. So they have an evil life that spiritually understood is a death.

The spirits who are with us—both those united to heaven and those united to hell—never flow into us from their own memory and consequent thought. If they did flow into us from their own thought it would seem to us exactly as though their character was our own. However, there does flow into us through them an affection from a love of what is good and true from heaven and an affection from a love of what is evil and false from hell. So to the extent that our own affection agrees with what is flowing in, we accept its influence in our thinking. This is because our more inward thought is in complete accord with our affection or love. To the extent that our own affection does not agree, we do not accept [the influence]. We can see from this that thoughts are not instilled into us by spirits but only an affection for what is good or an affection for what is evil. This gives us a choice because it gives us freedom. It means that in our thought we can accept what is good and reject what is evil, since we know from the Word what is good and what is evil. What we accept in thought from affection becomes part of us, while what we do not accept in thought from affection does not become part of us. This enables us to determine the nature of the inflow into us of the good from heaven and of the evil from hell.

I have been enabled to learn where we get the anxiety, distress of mind, and inward sadness called depression. There are spirits who are not yet united with hell because they are still in their first state [after death].They love half-digested and noxious substances like the foods that are becoming excrement in the stomach, so they attach themselves to the same sort of matter in us, because they find delight in it; and they talk with each other there out of their evil affection. The emotional tone of their conversation flows into us, and since it is contrary to our affection, it brings about a sadness and an anxious depression; while if it agrees with our affection, it brings about a sense of happiness and exhilaration. These spirits can be seen in the neighborhood of the stomach, some on the left and some on the right, some lower and some higher, nearer or farther away—variously depending on the affections they are involved in. A great deal of experience has convinced me that they are the source of our anxiety of spirit. I have seen them, heard them, felt the anxieties that well up from them. I have talked with them, they have been driven off and the anxiety has ceased, they have come back and the anxiety has returned, I have observed its increase and decrease as they drew near and moved away. It has become clear to me, then, where that anxiety originates that is blamed on a stomachache by people who do not know what conscience is because they do not have any. . . .

I have talked with angels about the union of heaven with the human race and have told them that church people actually do say that everything good is from the Lord and that there are angels with us, but few people really believe that angels are so close to us, much less that they are in our thought and affection. The angels have told me that they knew this kind of [empty] belief and talk occurred in the world, and especially (which astonished them) in the church, where people have the Word that teaches them about heaven and its union with them. Yet in fact the union is so vital that we could not think the least thought apart from the spirits who are with us. Our spiritual life depends on this. They said that the reason for this ignorance was that people believe they live on their own, without any connection with the Ultimate Reality of life, and do not know that there is this connection through the heavens. Yet if that connection were severed, we would instantly drop down dead. If we believed the way things really are, that everything good comes from the Lord and everything evil from hell, then we would not take credit for the good within us or blame for the evil. Whenever we thought or did anything good, we would focus on the Lord, and any evil that flowed in we would throw back into the hell it came from. But since we do not believe in any inflow from heaven or from hell and therefore believe that everything we think and intend is in us and from us, we make the evil our own and defile the good with our feeling that we deserve it.

Epilogue:
ETERNAL SPRINGTIME

THOSE WHO KNOW HOW TO SHARE love are constantly advancing into the springtime of their youth in heaven, and the more millennia they live, the more joyful and happy that springtime is. Their progress continues forever, its never-ending increase determined by their development and growth in the capacity for sharing love, in charity and in faith.

A woman who dies old, worn out by age, and who lived a life marked by [qualities such as] faith in the Lord, charity toward her neighbors, and a happy, loving marriage with her husband—such a woman develops more and more of the bloom of mid- and early womanhood with the passage of years. She takes on a loveliness that eclipses any conception of beauty ever seen by the eye. Virtue and kindness are what shape her and make her a likeness of themselves. They cause the joy and beauty of neighborly love to shine out from the smallest details of her face, so that she becomes a form of charity itself. Some observers have been struck speechless on seeing these women.

The inner workings of charity are such that charity itself is what provides the visible form and is the thing expressed in that form too. This is clear from actual experience in the other life. The whole angel, especially the face, is charity, which is both clearly presented to view and clearly perceived. To see the form is to see inexpressible beauty that touches the deepest, living reaches of the mind, filling them with charity. The beauty of the form provides an image in which religious truth is displayed—truth that is also perceived from that form.

Those who have lived a life marked by faith in the Lord, that is, by the faith that comes of charity, become these visible forms— these beauties—in the next life. All angels are such forms, in unlimited variety. Of them heaven is made.

Sources

THE EXCERPTS FROM Emanuel Swedenborg's works that appear in this book were taken from three sources:

- *Heaven and Hell* (originally published in Latin as *De Coelo et Ejus Mirabilibus, et de Inferno, ex Auditis et Visis,* 1758) is a systematic description of heaven, hell, and the world of spirits in between, including a detailed description of what happens to us after death. The passages in this work are taken from a translation by George F. Dole (West Chester, PA: Swedenborg Foundation, 2002).

- *Marriage Love* (*Delitiae Sapientiae de Amore Conjugiali, Post Quas Sequuntur Voluptates Insaniae De Amore Scortatorio,* 1768) is Swedenborg's description of the relationship between the sexes, from not only an earthly standpoint but a spiritual one as well. Written in an era and cultural context very different from the present day, the volume as a whole may present challenges for a modern audience, but it also offers a fascinating perspective on marriage in the afterlife. The passages in this volume are taken from an unpublished translation by George F. Dole.

- *Secrets of Heaven* (*Arcana Coelestia,* 1749–56), Swedenborg's first published theological work, was also his longest, consisting of eight Latin volumes in its original edition. The bulk of the work is a verse-by-verse description of the inner meaning of Genesis and Exodus, but interspersed with the Bible commentary are chapters that describe the nature of the spiritual realms. The excerpts in this work are taken from *Secrets of Heaven,* vols. 1–2, translated by Lisa Hyatt Cooper (West Chester, PA: Swedenborg Foundation, 2010–12).

Some passages in this volume have been edited for length, and some cross-references to Swedenborg's other writings have been removed. If you are interested in reading this material in its original context, refer to the sources listed below. Note that the references below cite section numbers rather than page numbers; the section numbers are from Swedenborg's original editions and are uniform across all translations.

"The Joys of Heaven": *Marriage Love* 1–10
"There are Three Heavens": *Heaven and Hell* 29–40
"Space in Heaven": *Heaven and Hell* 191–99
"Time in Heaven": *Heaven and Hell* 162–69
"Communities in Heaven": *Heaven and Hell* 41–50
"Angels' Homes": *Heaven and Hell* 183–90
"Amazing Sights in Heaven": *Secrets of Heaven* 1532–33;
    1620–32
"Angels' Clothing": *Heaven and Hell* 177–82
"What Angels Do": *Heaven and Hell* 387–94
"Married Partners after Death": *Marriage Love* 45–53
"A Wedding in Heaven": *Marriage Love* 19–20
"Sex in Heaven": *Marriage Love* 44

"Spiritual Perception and Auras": *Secrets of Heaven* 1383–99;
 1504–20

"The Language of Angels": *Heaven and Hell* 234–45

"How Angels Talk with Us": *Heaven and Hell* 246–57

"We Are Always in Contact with Heaven and Hell": *Heaven and Hell* 291–302

"Eternal Springtime": *Secrets of Heaven* 553

About Emanuel Swedenborg

EMANUEL SWEDENBORG (1688–1772) was born Emanuel Swedberg (or Svedberg) in Stockholm, Sweden, on January 29, 1688 (Julian calendar). He was the third of the nine children of Jesper Swedberg (1653–1735) and Sara Behm (1666–1696). At the age of eight he lost his mother. After the death of his only older brother ten days later, he became the oldest living son. In 1697 his father married Sara Bergia (1666–1720), who developed great affection for Emanuel and left him a significant inheritance. His father, a Lutheran clergyman, later became a celebrated and controversial bishop, whose diocese included the Swedish churches in Pennsylvania and in London, England.

After studying at the University of Uppsala (1699–1709), Emanuel journeyed to England, Holland, France, and Germany (1710–1715) to study and work with leading scientists in western Europe. Upon his return he apprenticed as an engineer under the brilliant Swedish inventor Christopher Polhem (1661–1751). He gained favor with Sweden's King Charles XII (1682–1718), who gave him a salaried position as an overseer of Sweden's mining industry (1716–1747). Although he was engaged, he never married.

After the death of Charles XII, Emanuel was ennobled by Queen Ulrika Eleonora (1688–1741), and his last name was changed to Swedenborg (or Svedenborg). This change in status gave him a seat in the Swedish House of Nobles, where he remained an active participant in the Swedish government throughout his life.

A member of the Swedish Royal Academy of Sciences, he devoted himself to scientific studies and philosophical reflections that culminated in a number of publications, most notably a comprehensive three-volume work on mineralogy (1734) that brought him recognition across Europe as a scientist and philosopher. After 1734 he redirected his research and publishing to a study of anatomy in search of the interface between the soul and body, making several significant discoveries in physiology.

From 1743 to 1745 he entered a transitional phase that resulted in a shift of his main focus from science and philosophy to theology. Throughout the rest of his life he maintained that this shift was brought about by Jesus Christ, who appeared to him, called him to a new mission, and opened his perception to a permanent dual consciousness of this life and the life after death.

He devoted the last decades of his life to studying Scripture and publishing eighteen theological titles that draw on the Bible, reasoning, and his own spiritual experiences. These works present a Christian theology with unique perspectives on the nature of God, the spiritual world, the Bible, the human mind, and the path to salvation.

Swedenborg died in London on March 29, 1772, at the age of eighty-four.